AT RISK

Susan Honeyman, Series Editor

AT
RISK

Black Youth and the Creative Imperative
in the Post-Civil Rights Era

Jennifer Griffiths

University Press of Mississippi / Jackson

The University Press of Mississippi is the scholarly publishing agency of
the Mississippi Institutions of Higher Learning: Alcorn State University,
Delta State University, Jackson State University, Mississippi State University,
Mississippi University for Women, Mississippi Valley State University,
University of Mississippi, and University of Southern Mississippi.

www.upress.state.ms.us

The University Press of Mississippi is a member
of the Association of University Presses.

Copyright © 2023 by University Press of Mississippi
All rights reserved

First printing 2023

∞

Library of Congress Cataloging-in-Publication Data

Names: Griffiths, Jennifer L., 1968– author.
Title: At risk : Black youth and the creative imperative in the post-civil
rights era / Jennifer Griffiths.
Other titles: Cultures of childhood.
Description: Jackson : University Press of Mississippi, 2023. | Series:
Cultures of childhood | Includes bibliographical references and index.
Identifiers: LCCN 2022040068 (print) | LCCN 2022040069 (ebook) | ISBN
9781496841704 (hardcover) | ISBN 9781496841711 (trade paperback) | ISBN
9781496841728 (epub) | ISBN 9781496841735 (epub) | ISBN 9781496841742
(pdf) | ISBN 9781496841759 (pdf)
Subjects: LCSH: Creative ability in adolescence. | Creative ability in
children. | Gifted children—Education—United States. | At-risk
youth—United States. | Youth, Black—United States. | Youth with social
disabilities—United States. | Children of minorities—Education—United
States. | African American students. | African Americans—Education.
Classification: LCC BF724.3.C73 G75 2023 (print) | LCC BF724.3.C73
(ebook) | DDC 153.3/508996073—dc23/eng/20221014
LC record available at https://lccn.loc.gov/2022040068
LC ebook record available at https://lccn.loc.gov/2022040069

British Library Cataloging-in-Publication Data available

To Rody and Helaine, always and forever

CONTENTS

ix   Acknowledgments

3   Introduction

13   **CHAPTER 1** "On the Verge of Flying Back": The Problematic of the Young, Gifted, and Black Artist in Bill Gunn's *Johnnas*

45   **CHAPTER 2** "My Portrait Is Gold": Resiliency and the Crisis of the Black Child's Image in Dael Orlandersmith's *The Gimmick*

79   **CHAPTER 3** Posttraumatic Literacies and the Material Body in Sapphire's *Push*

119   **CHAPTER 4** "My Body of a Free Boy . . . My Body of Dance": Violence and the Choreography of Survival in Sapphire's *The Kid*

143   **CHAPTER 5** "You're Young, You're Black, and You're on Trial. What Else Do They Need to Know?": Reading Walter Dean Myers's *Monster*

175   Epilogue

177   Bibliography

187   Index

ACKNOWLEDGMENTS

My gratitude feels simple and direct, so this section will reflect that feeling. Thanks to my family and friends. Thanks to my colleagues at New York Institute of Technology. Thanks to Katie Keene, Camille Hale, Valerie Jones, Todd Lape, and the rest of the wonderful team at University Press of Mississippi. Thank you all.

An earlier version of chapter 4 was published as "'My body of a free boy . . . My body of dance': Violence and the Choreography of Survival in Sapphire's *The Kid*." *Obsidian: Literature in the African Diaspora,* vol. 13, no. 2 (2012).

AT RISK

INTRODUCTION

Being labeled "at risk" is like being voted least likely to succeed. For where there is no faith in your future success, there is no real effort to prepare you for it.
—Carol Brunson Day, *Being Black Is Not a Risk Factor: A Strengths-Based Look at the State of the Black Child.* National Black Child Development Institute (NBCDI)

In *Black Power to Hip Hop: Racism, Nationalism, and Feminism*, Patricia Hill Collins alludes to this generation's particular paradox: "Coming to adulthood after the decline of the civil rights and Black Power movements of the 1950s and 1960s, contemporary Black youth grew up during a period of initial promise, profound change, and, for far too many, heart-wrenching disappointment" (3). During the midcentury civil rights era, the most compelling images, the ones that captured a generation's struggle and awakened a nation to embrace radical change toward equality for all, involved Black youth facing unmitigated racial hatred. A tiny Ruby Bridges surrounded by guards, the school photos of four little girls from Birmingham, and the disfigured face of a fourteen-year-old Chicago boy in an open casket—these images remain indelible in our collective imagination. The violence—spiritual, psychological, and physical—directed toward Black youth served as a catalyst for action. As Katharine Capshaw puts it: "Picturing childhood became a powerful instrument of civil rights activism, because children carry an important aura of human value and potential, and threats to the young made the stakes of the movement palpable to individuals and to the nation. Undoubtedly, images of children under siege had generative effects for the civil rights campaign" (xi). In the post–civil rights era, including notably our current moment, we have new images with which to grapple, including the videotaped shootings of Latasha Harlins and Tamir Rice, the school-photo collage of the Atlanta Child Murder victims, and the family photos of Michael Brown and Trayvon Martin. The interpretation of most of these contemporary images is hotly contested with unrelenting immediacy, illuminating the critical changes between the earlier period and the current one. Although hypervisible, the Black child's violated body does not have the same rhetorical position in the political climate of contemporary America, due in part to the disconnectedness and belatedness characterizing posttraumatic experience.

In a think-piece for the online journal *The Conversation*, Howard University professor Ivory A. Toldson calls for changing a practice that labels more than identifies: "When students are labeled 'at-risk,' it serves to treat them as a problem because of their risk factors. Instead, students' unique experiences and perspectives should be normalized, not marginalized. This reduces a problem known as 'stereotype threat,' a phenomenon in which students perform worse academically when they are worried about living up to a negative stereotype about their group" ("Why It's Wrong to Label Students 'At Risk'"). *At Risk* focuses on representations of Black artists as adolescents as they develop strategies to intervene against the stereotypes that threaten to limit their horizons. Through their creative experiments, they capture and convey the complex experience of this specific generation's young people, paying specific attention to what it means to be deemed "at risk" and narrowed within the scope of a sociological problem, all while trying to expand the horizons of creative possibility.

At Risk includes chapters focusing on the following primary texts: Sapphire's *Push* and *The Kid*, Walter Dean Myers's *Monster*, Dael Orlandersmith's *The Gimmick*, and Bill Gunn's *Johnnas*, and through a close character analysis and synthesis with cultural and historical perspectives, the study hopes to expand scholarly work on race, childhood, resiliency, and trauma studies. The five texts examined within provide representations of Black gifted children, child artists who find themselves faced within their identity formation and the sense of being both hypervisible and invisible. They each come to terms with their "at risk" status within their art and address the ways that they experience the "at risk" label that threatens to narrow their existence at a moment when they need to take risks, to question, and to make questionable choices without overly harsh consequences.

Risk has unique and layered meanings within discourses connected to the culture wars, posttraumatic response, and creative imperative. *At Risk* considers the ways in which the literary and cultural possibilities of the period allow for a more honest, multilayered, and forthright depiction of Black youth subjectivity and the negotiation of racialization, asking, "What do these literary texts offer us when we consider the transitional post–civil rights period through the lens of a transitional stage in individual development?" A great deal of social science research exists on their "at risk" lives, with titles such as *Young, Black, and Male in America: An Endangered Species* (1988) amplifying the potentially harmful aspects of life for youth of color. *At Risk: Black Youth and the Creative Imperative in the Post–Civil Rights Era* seeks a greater focus on the agency to resist labels by working with literary texts that place limiting social, historical, and linguistic paradigms "at risk" and present leaps to resilience and possibility in their place. It serves alongside existing efforts, such as Cathy Cohen's *Black Youth Project* (http://research.blackyouthproject.com/) and Shawn Ginwright's *Black Youth Rising: Activism and Radical Healing in Urban America*, and adds a consideration of literary efforts to raise critical questions and flesh out complexities in representations of Black youth in the recent US culture.

Adolescence has long been viewed as a period of risk by the culture at large, and current neuroscience research indicates that teens' increased propensity for risk accompanies a necessary period of cognitive and emotional development. In his 2011 *National Geographic* piece "Beautiful Brains," David Dobbs describes recent research into adolescence to explain their evolutionary relationship to risk:

> So if teens think as well as adults do and recognize risk just as well, why do they take more chances? Here, as elsewhere, the problem lies less in what teens lack compared with adults than in what they have more of. Teens take more risks not because they don't understand the dangers but because they weigh risk versus reward differently.... In situations where risk can get them something they want, they value the reward more heavily than adults do.

Teens "value the reward more" because they need the novelty to explore and adapt to their future life stage as adults and are "hardwired" to seek new ways to expand their capacities. Dobbs's examination of the current studies confirms that "this risk-friendly weighing of cost versus reward has been selected for because, over the course of human evolution, the willingness to take risks during this period of life has granted an adaptive edge. Succeeding often requires moving out of the home and into less secure situations." However, this necessary risk-taking becomes particularly fraught when considering the ways Black youth face racialized inscription that deems their growing bodies as less safe or as a threat to public safety. In "Criminalizing Normal Adolescent Behavior in Communities of Color: The Role of Prosecutors in Juvenile Justice Reform," Kristin Henning posits:

> Over the last quarter century, psychological research has shown that much of youth crime and delinquency is the product of normal adolescent development. Compared to adults, adolescents

often make impetuous and ill-considered decisions, are susceptible to negative influences and outside pressures, and have a limited capacity to identify and weigh the short- and long-term consequences of their choices. (385)

In other words, there is very little room for Black youth to experiment and engage in the necessary risk taking without placing themselves "at risk" in perilous ways.

In addition, another type of risk is connected specifically to trauma, when young people cope with the unresolved issues from abuse or neglect at a familial or societal level with risky behavior that distracts and substitutes a temporarily positive sensation for the hurt that may threaten to overwhelm. Conversely, the posttraumatic experience often also includes a kind of emotional and even physiological constriction that results in risk-aversive behaviors with a constriction of emotional range. There is the "social problem" aspect of "at risk" that implies that a subject requires outside intervention by agencies, institutions, and the state to survive. The very institutions that label Black children "at risk" foster situations that traumatize or retraumatize with policies that reveal unexamined racism as scholars such as Dorothy Roberts have uncovered about child welfare systems.

In *At Risk*, the child artists take these systems and place them under close scrutiny within their painterly or writerly productions, and this way, they employ the risk-taking of divergent thinking that has been recognized as a hallmark of creativity. There is also the association of risk with creativity, including the research on divergent thinking, and research has long established the link between adolescence and creativity with "findings from a 25-year research project on creative thinking indicat[ing] that the development of creative capacity occurs primarily during the adolescent period" (Rothenberg).

Chapter 1, "On the Verge of Flying Back": The Problematic of the Young, Gifted, and Black Artist in Bill Gunn's *Johnnas*," raises the issue of artistic giftedness in Black youth as a problematic articulated in Bill Gunn's 1968 play *Johnnas*. Johnnas remains an outcast in his brief life, in spite of tremendous potential, when he fails to find the kind of artistic community essential for reconciling his work with identity, culture, and history. In his foreword essay "Sweet Lorraine," James Baldwin introduces Lorraine Hansberry's *To Be Young, Gifted, and Black* with tribute to his late friend, and in this tribute, he describes Hansberry's struggles with finding an artistic home in twentieth-century America as a Black woman. In his discussion of Hansberry, Baldwin raises central concerns about Black artists, ones that relate to Bill Gunn's depiction of the struggling Johnnas:

> This country's concept of art and artists has the same effect, scarcely worth mentioning by now, of isolating the artist from the people. One can see the effect of this in the irrelevance of so much of the work produced by white artists; the effect of this isolation on a black artist is absolutely fatal. He *is*, already, as a black American citizen, isolated from most of his artistic peers for help, for they do not know enough about him to be able to correct him. To continue to grow, to remain in touch with himself, he needs the support of that community from which, however, all of the pressures of American life incessantly conspire to remove him. And when he is effectively removed, he falls silent—and the people have lost another hope. (xviii–xix)

Johnnas serves as an introduction to the problematic of the "young, gifted, and Black" artist presented in Gunn's complex representation at a critical threshold in relation to the civil rights era.

The subsequent chapters center on adolescent creativity within a post–civil-rights-era urban landscape that encapsulates many issues, most notably parental neglect, addiction, abuse, teenage pregnancy, foster care, and criminal activity, which accompany the "at-risk" designation. Chapter 2, "'My Portrait Is Gold': Resiliency and the Crisis of the Black Child's Image in Dael Orlandersmith's *The Gimmick*," addresses the explicit black adolescent body in the visual realm, both as a legacy and a cultural phenomenon that recurs in the time of the play's initial production.

In the third chapter, "Posttraumatic Literacies and the Material Body in Sapphire's *Push*," the analysis amplifies the moment in Sapphire's *Push* when Precious sits in the classroom, and Ms. Rain asks the students to introduce themselves. Precious shares that this experience—of self-reflecting and listening within the classroom—is new to her. Ms. Rain asks how she feels, to which Precious responds, "Here." In this direct declaration of presence, Precious occupies her body in the small student desk and claims an integrated self in the "here." The moment gestures toward a commitment to experiencing her presence in her own body and to anchoring her connection to past bodies through intertextuality related to a Black literary canon.

Chapter 4, "'My Body of a Free Boy . . . My Body of Dance': Violence and the Choreography of Survival in Sapphire's *The Kid*," examines Sapphire's *The Kid* as a radical experiment with audience expectations and reception of her first novel *Push*. Whereas *Push*'s Precious Jones was embraced by many audiences as a model of resiliency and as a young person who breaks the cycle of abuse through education, self-determination, and group-belonging, Abdul's story threatens our comfort with his mother's ultimately reassuring narrative, which in many ways deflects accountability away from the failing social safety net and onto the individual. Described as "misery porn," *The Kid* never yields to the audience desire for certain uplift and establishes a new code of resiliency on its own terms. This chapter explores the narrative strategies that allow for a sustained engagement with the constant and cumulative traumatic experience of an African American AIDS orphan as he enters a period of self-definition in adolescence. It considers how the novel contrasts institutionalized foster care and social service interventions with artistic expression and a search for personal and cultural histories to replace the damaging state surrogates. Adolescence marks a time of departure and a coming into power for Abdul when he can no longer remain in state care. The reception of his body also transforms in adolescence from vulnerable to threatening, which results in his removal from the Catholic boy's home. He discovers his true home within dance, and within this site of reunion between body and memory, he creates unconventional, ragged possibilities for survival.

In the wake of the Michael Brown shooting in Ferguson, Missouri, a Black Twitter campaign emerged that responded to selective circulation of images suggesting the criminality of Black youth. Using the hashtag #iftheygunnedmedown, this social media protest included two seemingly disparate images: one that would be construed as "thug-like" behavior and one with normative, positive images, including graduation and family photos. The campaign recalls the "iamtrayvonmartin" campaign on Tumblr in which people dressed up wearing black hoodies.

Chapter 5, "'You're Young, You're Black, and You're on Trial. What Else Do They Need to Know?': Reading Walter Dean Myers's *Monster*," compares recent social media efforts to reclaim the self-representation of Black youth with Walter Dean Myers's novel *Monster*, an experimental text in which an African American teenager scripts his experience in jail and on trial for a murder he did not commit. In both experimental texts, young Black men take control of their images and critique the criminalization and dehumanization they face in relation to criminalization of Black youth. Part of the analysis will include the recent exoneration of the Central Park Five and will compare Myers's novel with the depiction of the five teenagers in the Central Park case, who were all treated as "monsters" in the court of public opinion. With this history and current critique in mind, this chapter will examine *Monster* as a radical creative intervention toward recognizing the complex, nuanced subjectivity of a young Black man who takes control over his own narrative under extreme circumstances.

The texts included in *At Risk* contribute to an intervention in institutions that reinforce the "at risk" characterization of Black youth. Each text also most notably centers around an individual young Black artist's exploration of their racialized identity and artistic development. There are concrete engagements with the process of artistic creation. All reflect the development of a critical consciousness of oneself and one's relationship to institutions, society, and culture as the characters examine their artistic inspirations and process often in harrowing circumstances. In addition, although risk may not always be explicitly named, the characters have a sense of themselves as objects of public scrutiny, and they confront the narrowing of their potential as creative subjects and place their objectification as "at-risk" through their intentional crafting of other possibilities in their art.

CHAPTER 1

"ON THE VERGE OF FLYING BACK"

The Problematic of the Young, Gifted, and Black Artist in Bill Gunn's *Johnnas*

A children's story I wrote speaks of a black male child that dreamed of a strong white golden haired prince who would come and save him from being black. He came, and as time passed and the relationship moved forward, it was discovered that indeed the black child was the prince and he had saved himself from being white. That, too, is possible.
—Bill Gunn, "To Be a Black Artist"

At Risk begins by examining artistic giftedness in Black youth as a problematic articulated in Bill Gunn's 1968 play *Johnnas*. As a noun, "problematic" appears less often, but here it gestures to incorporate the W. E. B. DuBois's well-known reflection on Blackness and double-consciousness that "being a problem is a strange experience" (7) when he reflects on "this sense of always looking at one's self through the eyes of others, of measuring one's soul by the tape of a world that looks on in amused contempt and pity" (8) while also examining a particular set of issues or concerns both within and outside of community that face developing Black artists within the post–civil rights era. The young artist Johnnas remains an outcast in his brief life, in spite of tremendous potential, when he fails to find the kind of artistic community essential for reconciling his work with identity, culture, and history. In his foreword essay "Sweet Lorraine," James Baldwin introduces Lorraine Hansberry's *To Be Young, Gifted, and Black* with a tribute to his late friend, and in this tribute, he describes Hansberry's struggles with finding an artistic home in twentieth-century America as a Black woman. Throughout his discussion of Hansberry, Baldwin raises central concerns about Black artists, ones that relate to Bill Gunn's depiction of the struggling Johnnas:

> This country's concept of art and artists has the same effect, scarcely worth mentioning by now, of isolating the artist from the people. One can see the effect of this in the irrelevance of so much of the work produced by white artists; the effect of this isolation on a black artist is absolutely fatal. He is, already, as a black American citizen, isolated from most of his artistic peers for help, for they do not know enough about him to be able to correct him. To continue to grow, to remain in touch with himself, he needs the support of that community from which, however, all of the pressures of American life incessantly conspire to remove him. And when he is effectively removed, he falls silent—and the people have lost another hope. (xviii)

Published in 1968 in *TDR: The Drama Review*'s special issue on Black theater, *Johnnas* positions a portrait of the artist as a Black child at the issue's center and seems to respond to Baldwin's assertion that "the effect of this isolation on a black artist is absolutely fatal." The play begins with an actor speaking both as Johnnas and as "The Judge," recounting the story of his parents' relationship, which involved their early days as musicians and performers. The play culminates in Johnnas's suicide, raising compelling questions about this ultimate act's connection to his creative trajectory, his experience of his possibilities, and the tensions between integration and isolation for the Black artist. Near the play's end, when Johnnas responds to the crowd's cries for him to "Jump" from the building he has ascended, he presents the audience with the paradox of the clear hopelessness of this self-annihilating act and the freedom he grasps for in this desperate leap beyond the forces that attempt to over-determine his life. As the hole at the special issue's center, his suicide positions Johnnas between politics and art at this critical moment, 1968, and its place in the post–civil rights era as a transitional period in defining Black art and African American life. The crisis includes the struggles between the individual and the collective, particularly when defining Black artists and the cost or failed promises of integration for the gifted Black child. Gunn's short play serves as a bridge between past and contemporary issues that remain relevant, and this chapter will examine the play in conversation with cultural productions and interdisciplinary research that raise questions about creativity, precarity, and the Black child.

The issue's guest editor, Ed Bullins, begins his introductory piece "The King Is Dead," which refers to the impact of Martin Luther King Jr.'s recent assassination on the issue and the state of Black theater, with a quotation by Floyd McKissick, national director of the Congress of Racial Equality (CORE) from 1966 to 1968: "Dr. Martin Luther King was the last prince of nonviolence. He was a symbol of nonviolence, the epitome of nonviolence. Nonviolence is a dead philosophy and it was not the black people that killed it" (qtd. in Bullins 23). In his introduction to the issue, Bullins describes his experience the night of the King assassination. He was at St. Mark's Playhouse to see a Wole Soyinka play with the Negro Ensemble Company and felt compelled to consider ongoing questions about the relationship between politics and art for the Black community as he "wondered at that moment about those Black theatre people who profess not to be concerned about politics, or 'just let their Blackness speak for itself'" (24). The special issue stands at a critical moment in the struggle for racial justice when optimism and faith meet a crisis. Younger people led this moment's transition into a more revolutionary, less reform-oriented program. Aligning with the sentiments expressed by McKissick, Stokely Carmichael's well-known words mark the moment as experienced by many young people:

> Dr. King's policy was that nonviolence would achieve the gains for black people in the United States. His major assumption was that if you are nonviolent, if you suffer, your opponent will see your suffering and will be moved to change his heart. That's very good. He only made one fallacious assumption: In order for nonviolence to work, your opponent must have a conscience. The United States has none. (*The Black Power Mixtape*)

Carmichael's words echo the realization for many activists that the pathos appeal advanced through the photography, speeches, and narratives of the 1950s and early 1960s no longer seemed relevant or efficacious at this critical juncture. What does that mean for the young Black artist who must shatter the constraints of the child-as-symbol?

Embodying "young, gifted, and Black" at this historical moment, the character of Johnnas emerges from the scene of previous struggle over the child figure within the civil rights movement, particularly involving violent resistance to integration. The images that resonate most powerfully in the collective memory around the civil rights gains in mid-century and that appear to serve as a catalyst for change include Black youth facing violent backlash and retaliation for gaining proximity to whiteness in schools and other public spaces, including most notably Ruby Bridges and the Little Rock Nine's Elizabeth Eckford encountering malicious resistance to their entrance into previously white-only classrooms. After crossing these hostile thresholds, Black children clearly faced struggles with assimilation into white-dominated institutions that have anti-Blackness sewn into the fabric of their formation and sustenance. In other spaces, Black and brown youth released anger in the streets. In the *The Drama Review* volume, the majority of the anger is directed outward, and expressions of revolution intend to overthrow institutions that advance white supremacy; however, *Johnnas* offers a different take when the young Black artist turns on himself, suggesting the unresolved internal conflict between individual and collective identity, particularly for the artist.

Johnnas represents both the struggle to integrate and the resistance to it in relation to Black youth, and Gunn's experiences may have shaped the critical questions he raises in this important work that deserves renewed attention. Steve Ryfle describes Bill Gunn's middle-class upbringing as notably similar to Johnnas's life:

> Gunn was born July 15, 1929 to William Harrison Gunn Sr. and Louise Alexander and grew up in a mostly white, middle-class section of West Philly. His father was a singer, songwriter, comedian, and poet who had worked with blues vocalists Bessie Smith and Ma Rainey; his mother was an actress and ran a theater company. Gunn was educated in integrated public schools and encouraged by his parents to read and act; he felt the sting of racism in his hometown, but, "he said his family raised him as if he were white and middle class," said longtime friend Chiz Schultz, producer of The Angel Levine and Ganja & Hess. "Bill didn't feel he'd been brought up as an African-American man." (27)

Early in Gunn's career, he performed in Louis S. Peterson's *Take a Giant Step* in an off-Broadway production of the play, which focuses on the isolation of Spence, a Black teen growing up in a predominantly white, middle-class environment. Spence's best confidante, Gram, dies shortly after she gives an impassioned speech to Spence's parents in which she admonishes them for failing to see their child's pain and loneliness. At the play's end, he says goodbye preemptively to his childhood friends with the realization that the relationships would not survive their passage into racially segregated adulthood. The one relationship that appears to have the ability to exist beyond childhood is with Alan, who wants to go to "State" college with Spence, where they will become "intellectuals," suggesting that becoming an intellectual will offer a window to a continuing connection between the friends. Both plays offer the sense that upward mobility presents its own traps for Black youth, who must resist efforts to keep them "in their place," referred to as "microaggressions" in twenty-first-century discussions. The play navigates the complex issue related to social mobility and adolescence, as young people need to separate from parents developmentally while also facing the realities of racism for Black teens. *Take a Giant Step* ends rather pragmatically with Spence appearing to come to terms with his new consciousness and changing relationships.

Like *Take a Giant Step*, *Johnnas* centers around life after integration and the achievement of middle-class life. It stands outside the issues raised in the controversial "The Negro Family, The Case for National Action" (1965), or known also as the "Moynihan Report" after Assistant Secretary of Labor Daniel Patrick Moynihan. The report from Office of Policy Planning and Research, United States Department of Labor offered a directive toward "a new kind of national goal: the establishment of a stable Negro family structure" to counter what the report identifies as "the fundamental source of the weakness of the Negro community at the present time." The report asserts,

> There is probably no single fact of Negro American life so little understood by whites. The Negro situation is commonly perceived by whites in terms of the visible manifestation of discrimination and poverty, in part because Negro protest is directed against such obstacles, and in part, no doubt, because these are facts which involve the actions and attitudes of the white community as well. It is more difficult, however, for whites to perceive the effect that three centuries of exploitation have had on the fabric of Negro society itself. Here the consequences of the historic injustices done

to Negro Americans are silent and hidden from view. But here is where the true injury has occurred: unless this damage is repaired, all the effort to end discrimination and poverty and injustice will come to little. (Geary)

In *Johnnas*, Gunn represents a similar family structure. While this report posits the breakdown of the Black family as a central factor that undermines Black success, *Johnnas* counters this conclusion by exposing the challenges faced by the gifted Black child, even when the family of origin is intact and functioning as a cohesive unit. The focus is returned to the external forces of racism—as well as the community byproducts—that constrict this burgeoning artist. The backlash against this report is well documented and objected primarily to the lack of focus on systemic and institutionalized conditions that continued to hinder African American life.

Johnnas offers a response to complicate the Moynihan report within the context of this 1968 crisis. Integration and heteronormative family structures do not automatically guarantee the necessary conditions for the young Black artist to thrive in freedom, and *Johnnas* raises these inadequacies at a time when hope is so tenuous after King's assassination in the *TDR* issue focusing on Black revolutionary theater in 1968, which includes other work with messages of radicalism over reform and Afrocentric worldviews. If as Kate Capshaw describes "childhood as an icon of both the Black nation and in generative processes of development" (Introduction, *Civil Rights Childhood*), then how does Bill Gunn's short play *Johnnas*, which culminates in the suicide of a young, gifted, and Black writer reflect its moment corresponds to a crisis in hope? The *TDR* issue explores the tension between integration and assimilation and its relationship to art, particularly through the figure of the child artist Johnnas, whose mother identifies as embodying an inherent risk and vulnerability:

> He's such a sensitive child. I say to Barney that he has a fragile soul. It seems always on the verge of flying back. Barney thinks he should make an effort to get along with the other children, but he doesn't understand that the other children don't care whether he is with them or not, and Johnnas misses his books and his writing. He should not be made to neglect them for these other children who don't care if he is dead or alive. (134)

In this context, it becomes tricky to interpret his final act. Is his suicide a radical gesture to reject the impossible limitations placed on the Black artists within white supremacy? Perhaps outside the context of the issues itself, the play would be forced into a demoralized reading. It would signal hopelessness. Within this *TDR* issue that amplifies radical voices, including Jimmy Garrett's *And We Own the Night*, with its revolutionary youth committing matricide to destroy distractions, *Johnnas* stands apart in its representation of intergenerational connection, yet these relationships do not allow Johnnas to choose to remain in this life, which seems counter to the resistance offered in the issue's other work. Is his suicide part of a sacrifice legitimized within revolutionary rhetoric and ethos, or does it raise questions about the struggles for artists to navigate identity and politics in relation to creative freedom?

Johnnas connects generations and creative legacies by including the stories of his parents, Barney and Hilly, both artists who traveled through white spaces, who also remain throughout the play centrally supportive of their son, even as they harbor anxiety and fear for his life as a young Black artist. An adult actor speaking as Johnnas opens the play and begins to tell his father's story. It is the story of art and survival, and the father-artist uses his creative gifts to navigate the segregated south in the first half of the twentieth century. It is also a story of travel and movement/migration toward the promise of the north. As the Johnnas/Judge role narrates the father's story, the play raises intergenerational concerns also addressed within the *TDR* issue and in Gunn's other work, including the struggle to create space beyond the strictures of white supremacy and the impact of this legacy on new work. In "Black Theatre: Present Condition," Woodie King Jr. asks, "Why must each new generation of black artists suffer the faults of the past generation? . . . History is being ignored; a knowledge of the people is needed" (118–19) and asserts that "a black who works in the theatre, who cannot survive without it, can easily go out of his mind trying to write about it" (117). King Jr. offers a stark description of Black artists' predicament: "A majority of the young black artists are fed up with the way white people are stealing black art. They are very angry with the black pimps and hustlers. Some see no hope and slash their wrists, thus ending it all. A few stopped talking a long time ago. They stare. Sometimes they smile simply like inmates in an asylum" (124). Gunn explores this central predicament throughout his work, although in later work, he presents characters struggling with the issues at a different stage in their artistic development. In Gunn's 1975 play *Black Picture Show*, a screenwriter-son introduces the play and his father's demise: "When he found out I was creative he cried and, in his effort, to unveil futility, he died" (3). Gunn continues to present the struggle between political accountability and artistic authenticity through the father-son dynamic in *Black Picture Show*. The father, Alexander, provides insight into this potential crisis of meaning when he speaks to his son J. D.: "Let me tell you something. My hands are tied . . . This is what I've come to. This is oblivion. It is the posture of my life . . . This is not art . . . this is politics! Politics is the excrement of power. Art is life. Politics is inanimate and dead! It is the hammer of persuasion. And your persuasion is art? Art is truth . . . *and truth lies bleeding under the hammer*" (65). In his *New York Times* review for the play's New York Shakespeare Festival opening, Clive Barnes refers to Gunn as "a splendid dramatic writer," while noting that Gunn presents tensions, rather than offering direct resolutions: "I take leave to question whether in 'Black

Picture Show' he has really come to terms with his material. But this is worth discussing." The entire point may be that Gunn has not—and refuses to—"come to terms with his material" because his material is the unsettledness of the Black artistic experience, particularly when viewed through an intergenerational dynamic. In *Black Picture Show*, Alexander's comments about his beliefs on art reflect a disconnect with politics, and his art/commerce relationship contributes to his death ultimately.

Steve Ryfle affirms Gunn's position as standing between diverse perspectives and that this nuance informed his work:

> Bill Gunn was a unique talent who fit into neither the mainstream nor the revolution. His work confronted America's black/white chasm in more subtle ways: his characters—like Gunn himself—were sophisticated, cultured, and educated; they surrounded themselves with middle- or upper-class trappings, engaged in interracial and same-sex relationships, and were often emotionally fragile or sensitive; they were aware of their African lineage but refused to be defined by race. (26).

Writing on the Black Film Center/Archive blog, writer Nicholas Forster observes that "Gunn hoped that he could work within a white supremacist industry and create art that revealed, as he told Janus Adams in a 1973 interview, 'the truth of my experience.'" It was a political cause but rarely articulated as such by the filmmaker who constantly stressed individuality. Working alongside but rarely with those tied to the Black Arts Movement, Gunn always found himself apart from that movement." Perhaps, however, asserting and reinforcing a place "apart from the movement" through his representations of artists, who more often than not met with an early death at their own hands, Gunn fleshed out a particular problematic inherent to the Black Arts/Black Power intellectual and creative project, as Raymond S. Franklin articulates in "The Political Economy of Black Power": "Black Power in its totality neither a separatist nor an integrationist doctrine, and therefore is not directly related to either narrow nationalist formulations of the past nor civil rights ones of the present. *It is an answer to the Negro dilemma of neither being able to separate nor integrate"* (292).

In Bill Gunn's best-known work, the vampire film *Ganga and Hess*, the Black artist as an adult commits suicide, indicating a recurring paradox explored by Gunn related to agency and expression for Black artistic liberation. The film's release itself became controversial in terms of Gunn's artistic control when the production company decided to release a version with edits not approved by Gunn; however, the original version captured the attention of critics for its artistry. The film, later re-released in its original state, including notably the relationship between an academic anthropologist, Dr. Hess Green, and complicated artist, George Meda, played by Gunn himself. After the artist figure commits suicide, Dr. Green uses his blood to sustain himself in the vampire life. Manthia Diawara and Phyllis R. Klotman describe the complex depiction of the Black artist:

> [Meda is] plagued by the problem of identity. He tells Green in a conversation that he is schizophrenic: Meda feels sometimes like a victim and sometimes like a murderer. Meda is literally the victim in the film; he is attacked by a vampire, Green. Meda, as a black artist in the U.S. is also a victim of the condition of racism: He cannot create, from a sociological standpoint, without accusing White America, but he also cannot create without involving Black America. (308)

As presented within the *TDR* special issue, a central concern Black theatre involved self-determination first, with integration and assimilation rejected for their self-undermining consequences, yet the Black revolutionary aesthetics of the time, with a call to collective identity also represents a struggle for the artist. In *Johnnas*, this problematic, which includes suicide as a meditation on impossibility, begins with a consideration of the character's generational legacy for both artistic limitations and family tragedies linked to the racism that dehumanizes the Black child.

Johnnas represents these intergenerational artistic concerns most notably through the story of Barney, Johnnas's father, and his experience with the cakewalk dance. As a popular theatrical form, the cakewalk included coded satire of white cultural practices and audiences and Barney performs this exaggerated dance that implicitly mocks the formality of white plantation culture while judged by a white audience for a prize cake. In "Rewriting the Body: Aida Overton Walker and the Social Formation of Cakewalking," David Krasner writes that the cakewalk is "a celebratory dance with links to both West African dance traditions and African American parody of white" and notes the cakewalk for its transgressive aspects, perhaps most significantly because it offered a creative vehicle for survival, as among "the first of the cultural forms to be used as a cross-over commodity, transgressing the racial divide" (Krasner 79). Champions at cakewalking were experts at parodying whiteness: "We see in that particular dance an exaggerated erectness and propriety, a mocking generality.... So we made fun of them in dance, and they [whites] thought 'Oh, the savages are attempting to imitate us'" (Cook qtd. in Krasner 80). The cakewalk provided further economic incentives when wealthy whites desired to learn the dance and paid for instruction from Black dancers. It marks a moment of Black art entering the marketplace and becoming monetized. Danielle Robinson notes, "The late 19th-century Cakewalk provides the first evidence I have located of African Americans teaching Black dancing for pay. Their clients were the fashionable elite of New York City" (26).

The cakewalk and its legacy remain a critical part of conversations around Black art and the white commercial audiences as exemplified most notably in Donald Glover's 2018 "This Is America," a song for which Glover, a.k.a. Childish Gambino, won a Record of the Year Grammy at a moment made ready for this critique by the Black Lives Matter movement. In her Blavity piece "Why I View Childish Gambino's 'This Is America' As Black Art Imitating White Fantasies," cultural critic Ida Harris remarks, "'This Is America" ain't about black folk. To me, it is black art imitating white fantasy vis-a-vis black reality. It is about white folks and the function of white supremacy specifically in how it negotiates blackness." Harris explains, "America consumes blackness and transforms it to benefit whiteness. In a country where whiteness reigns supreme, white people see black people as spectacle, as commerce, even worse as disposable. In nuanced fashion with this video, Gambino shows us these receipts from history and today." Rob Turner examines the song's video in relation to its cultural legacies and the enduring complexity of its layers: "The film has been dissected by an army of YouTube analysts, with freeze frames of Gambino set alongside grotesque cartoons from the Jim Crow South, blurring the rapper with a caricature from the Wilson era. The black performer is destabilised, yet again, by all these commentaries, as he is read (and re-read) in relation to both authentic self-expression and white pastiche." The video represents "an unresolved tension between sincerity and salesmanship hovers over the track. As Young Thug puts it, in the mysterious refrain that closes the film: 'You just a black man in this world / You just a barcode...'" "This Is America" offers a glimpse into the ongoing influence of this dynamic within Black cultural production and art-as-resistance.

Johnnas too connects the youth Black artist with the legacy of parody and commodification. The stage directions introduce the scene of the cake dance, when "music rises sharply and a bright spot comes on suddenly full blast on a large blown-up photo of a Negro couple dressed in the style of the late 1890s" (126). Reproducing spectacle, Barney uses his creativity to compose work that relies in many ways on his audience's misunderstanding of the coded commentary, which makes it as much rhetoric as art. Barney's success with the cakewalk introduces this artistic legacy as complicated by its dance with whiteness. However subversive the cakewalk may be in its enactment, it exists, for Barney, as a form awaiting an audience to appreciate its fullness. From within oppression, it was a way of resisting, but in the Black Arts Movement (BAM), the desire was for more direct rebellion and resistance.

Looking backward and assessing this legacy in his narration of his father's story, Johnnas observes that Barney, "the finest blues and scat singer of his day, the 1920s," who "Sang and knocked a glass off shelf with his notes" (126–27), Hilly reflects on Barney's optimism, even in the face of thwarted or unfulfilled artistic potential: "He was very good at song writing; he wrote wonderful songs. Well, some were not so good but the good ones were very good" (130). Barney's song-writing ability proved useful for his survival, and he sold a song titled "A Lovely Tree" for ten dollars in 1926 to pay a hotel bill. Within Barney's life, art remained in service and became a commodity to support his survival. He paid a price for these efforts to configure creative expression around the expectations of white audiences and forms that distorts the artist's freedom to express directly, as the narrator Johnnas observes: "The winning of one battle can leave you too disabled for the next. The first, leaving; the second, coming face to face with the ways of the world, this United States of America. America—to see one's self naked in the center of someone else's swimming pool, cold and without a life preserver. You are a genius at treading water, but you can't swim. . . . The Americans are so struck with amusement at your not being able to swim that they miss the beauty of your ability to survive. My father survived" (128). In Barney's lived version of "This Is America," the swimming pool invokes a larger metaphor for a Black body performing as spectacle, immersed in racism, a fluid intangible until the drowning. Treading water or swimming at all means successfully focusing one's energy and not panicking, which does not allow Barney, the artist, to sustain the position above the water. There is no real movement backward or forward, but Johnnas recognizes this ability as possessing beauty. In his observation, he names the external sources that create a spectacle and places his father's victory in context. The swimming pool is also a public space of segregation, and with this one analogy for his father's experience, Johnnas invokes a politics of pools and swimming related to African American life, one that contemporary Black cultural productions continue to address, such as in the 2016 "Sink or Swim" episode of Kenya Barris's popular sitcom *Black-ish* in which Dre Johnson, the family patriarch, reveals that he cannot swim. In the episode, his wife Rainbow also worries about being excluded from the neighbor's pool parties because of stereotypes about Black families not swimming. The episode shares the engagement with stereotypes around swimming and race: "Stereotypes suggest black people don't want to swim because they can't float, are scared of water and will do anything to avoid getting their hair wet. These widely held negative stereotypes are literally killing us. According to the Centers for Disease Control and Prevention, black children drown at 5.5 times the rate of other children. And in the United States, where 10 people drown every day, that is a lot of black lives lost" (Rosemond). Alongside these stereotypes exists the history of swimming pools and integration, including the specific incident and image that still circulates when hotel owners poured acid into pools with Black swimmers and drained the pool when Dorothy Dandridge dipped her toe into it. In more contemporary times, writer Hari Ziyad reflects on the historical implications of the 2015 McKinney pool incident, when a viral video circulated of a police officer pinning a fourteen-year-old African American girl on the ground after receiving a call about Black children swimming in a majority-white community pool:

> But pools unplagued by our bodies and the haunting flashbacks they bring have always occupied a special place in the white community's imagination. So much so that not too long ago they took specific care to ban us from them. Black skin was covered in a sickness that

was somehow benign enough for our mothers to nurse, hold and wipe the asses of their children at the expense of time with us, but as soon as our skin made contact with the water, the whole pool turned to filth. On a few occasions, throwing acid in the water as those same mothers swam was seen as a fitting punishment for molesting their pools, so many Black people can't swim because those who would have taught us were never allowed to learn how.

In his metaphor about white reception as prioritizing its "amusement at your not being able to swim," Johnnas witnesses his father, naked—vulnerable—immersed in waters with an amused but hostile audience, implying the way racism relies on a spectacle of suffering but does not allow for recognizing power in the ability to survive. The conditions under which his father expressed his artistic genius allowed for survival, in a chronic traumatic containment—like a swimming pool—not expansive. To tread water within a contained space designed to reinforce boundaries and limitations and spectacle, Johnnas notes, means that his father survived by adapting to the aesthetic forms that appealed to predominant conceptions of what a Black entertainer should do, with little room for Black artistic experimentation and movement. He improvises, educates himself, observes, and perfects, but there is no freedom to determine his way. The swimming pool also suggests a man-made container, associated with planned leisure. How does "treading water" here translate into artistic endeavors? What does it mean to tread water but not to swim? How can this part stand as a metaphor not only for Black life in America but for Black art? All of these questions about Johnnas's legacy factor significantly. "Beauty" is mentioned directly about his father's capacity to adapt and as Johnnas marks a space for an aesthetic of survival; however, in his own creative trajectory, Johnnas wants to fly.

The "JUMP" yelled at Johnnas by a crowd beneath the building on which he stood near the play's end indicates a turn away from his father's story and raises questions, when examined in relation to the pool comparison, about whether his suicide serves as a metaphor for the lack of choice and freedom faced by the young Black artist or a leap into another level that must emerge only through this radical gesture. Larry Neal remarks in "The Black Arts Movement":

> A main tenet of Black Power is the necessity for Black people to define the world in their own terms. The Black artist has made the same point in the context of aesthetics. The two movements postulate that there are in fact and in spirit two Americas—one black, one white. The Black artist takes this to mean that his primary duty is to speak to the spiritual and cultural needs of Black people. Therefore, the main thrust of this new breed of contemporary writers is to confront the contradictions arising out of the Black man's experience in the racist West. Currently, these writers are re-evaluating western aesthetics, the traditional role of the writer, and the social function of art. (29)

Johnnas presents an origin story for an artist growing up in this historical moment in which Neal's "new breed" of Black creativity emerges and responds to the contradictions in nuanced ways.

The story that Johnnas has inherited includes thwarted potential to engage in "high art" and elite cultural forms; Barney had the voice of an opera singer, but the possibility was not open to him (129). This narrowing of possibility recalls Nina Simone's expression of regret that she did pursue her passion to become a classical pianist. Gunn's longtime collaborator, Samuel Waymon, was Nina Simone's brother, and their shared home in Nyack, New York served as a creative hub in the 1970s for artists including Simone, Toni Morrison, and Amiri Baraka, and Simone's artistic struggles resonate throughout *Johnnas* in the questions the play raises about Black artists and freedom:

> In many ways, Nina Simone would shape the bulk of her career in response to an aesthetic conundrum: what should a black female artist sound like? Some of Simone's most famous song titles summed up this query. Through her music she sought to make her listeners grasp how "it would feel to be free" and to be "young, gifted, and black," as well as female. Her songs thus served as sonic struggles in and of themselves, as embattled efforts to elude generic categorizations as a black female performer. (Brooks 177)

Gunn presents this struggle through Johnnas, his understanding of his father's story, and the potential influence on his own trajectory as an artist.

In between the father Barney's story and his own struggle, another story is told that involves his mother, Hilly, and a trauma at the center of the family around birth and a crisis in hope. Hilly, Johnnas's mother and Barney's wife, also reflects on the limitations she faced as an artist: "In those days if you was a colored woman, you got married and raised your children, or did day work, cooked or went on the streets, or if you had the notion to travel and went on the stage, do anything, you could always work in the chorus. Or you could sing the blues that's all the white folks wanted to hear, or dance" (129). As a young musician and actor, Hilly had a contagious joy and found fellowship among legendary artists: "Bessie Smith used to come to Hilly and say, 'Hilly, give me that smile for luck.' Then on Bessie'd go and sing up some blues, and Hilly'd laugh" (129). However, the circumstances of Johnnas's birth reveal a fear and hopelessness about the Black child that reflects a profound shift in her spirit. Instead of serving as a figure of future, creativity, hope, Hilly-as-mother does not want to bear the unbearable again. Her terrible loss and its consequences speak in rejection to the external judgements manifested in the Moynihan Report. Hilly has a loving marriage and a middle-class life. Later, when Barney's employer asked Hilly if she would work in her kitchen, assuming she would be available for domestic work outside of her own home, Hilly replied that there was work enough in taking care of her own family (and Barney would not have been happy if he knew). However, since white supremacist medical practices had terrorized her first experience with motherhood, and upon learning about her second pregnancy, she remains unwilling to take the risk.

Hilly's story of loss occurs while the couple traveled in the old Ford to VA to visit Hilly's sister. Their toddler twins died of diphtheria after being seen by a white doctor who sent them away to find the Black doctor. Even when they returned extremely ill shortly after attempting to find the Black doctor, the white hospital would not treat, and to add to the bitterness, the physician began to examine the twins for treatment when he initially thought that Hilly was white. In her personal artistic journey, Hilly encountered trouble fitting into racialized schemas and was once offered a spot in a white touring company because she did not appear "black" enough: "she didn't have what he called colored quality." The doctor turns away critically ill young children when he sees the darker-skinned Black father, signifying that the medical oath and the societal expectation to protect children from harm does not apply in white supremacist worldview. If this essential piece is not taken care of in terms of the Black child in the world and in relation to white authority figures, how can the creative spirit find space to flourish? This connection between reproduction as risk is established through the death of the girl twins.

Hilly feels pregnant with impossibility when she learns that she will have another child. She reacts passionately, telling the doctor that she rejects this exposure to loss: "I DON'T WANT IT. YOU CAN'T MAKE ME HAVE IT! . . . I DON'T WANT TO BRING INTO THIS WORLD ANOTHER CHILD EVER AGAIN . . . EVER . . . EVER . . ." (132). Hilly responds unequivocally and rejects any attempts at "gaslighting" her: "Don't touch me. I'm not insane. It's just that I don't trust anyone to be good to my children" (132). Her new pregnancy returns her to the point when she encounters the previous doctor's failure to treat and to acknowledge the severity of the twins' illness, which reflects a pervasive and continuing issue regarding the medical racism and the failure of the medical establishment to view Black pain as valid and real. In current research, "findings suggest that individuals with at least some medical training hold and may use false beliefs about biological differences between blacks and whites to inform medical judgments, which may contribute to racial disparities in pain assessment and treatment" (Hoffman). Black children's physical pain often goes unrecognized, as the recent controversial study on pain medication and appendectomy exposes:

> Not surprisingly, as pain scores increased, the use of any analgesia (including opioid analgesia) increased overall. However, there appeared to be a threshold effect with respect to administration of analgesia by race. Black patients with moderate pain were less likely to receive any analgesia, and black patients with severe pain were less likely to be treated with opioids. This analysis by pain strata suggests that there may be a higher threshold of pain score for administering analgesia to black patients with appendicitis. (Goyal et al.)

Hilly's rejection of her pregnancy signals a radical disruption in the narrative that perpetuates that Black bodies remain impervious to pain. She claims her personal grief while connecting her trauma directly to the pervasive racism that has killed her babies and thwarted her desire to reproduce. "What is a Black Child?," Christina Sharpe asks in *In the Wake: On Blackness and Being*.

> In the United States, conservatives simultaneously call for an end to abortion and extoll the imagined virtues of it. Recall Bill Bennett, former Secretary of Education and "values czar": "If it is your sole purpose to reduce crime," Bennett said, "you could abort every black baby in this country, and your crime rate would go down." This is

The Problematic of the Young, Gifted, and Black Artist in *Johnnas* 33

execrable arithmetic, a violent accounting, another indication that the meaning of *child*, as it abuts blackness, falls . . . apart. (80)

Hilly's reaction reveals the ways in which she has learned directly about this "violent accounting," and she displays no interest in martyrdom. In this moment, we see that Hilly is unwilling to take the *risk of bringing a Black child into this world*. It is an extreme moment but one that also is naked and clear with little ambiguity and indirectness. Hilly represents a consciousness grounded in lived reality of loss and trauma. She experienced the helplessness of seeing her children's humanity stripped when their suffering goes unrecognized.

After Hilly's encounter with the Doctor who refused to abort Johnnas, the stage direction presents an adult Johnnas: "*She leaves quickly. The lights fade. The lights come up on a negro in his 30's, sitting at a tall school desk. This is* JOHNNAS" (132). Johnnas's journey as a new generation Black artist "Then his mother said he started crying at 12 and never stopped" (132). The merging of the narrative voice and the young Johnnas offers a connection between Gunn's play and the other pieces within the volume, which reflect the struggles of later adolescence and young adulthood in a time of radical cultural shifts. To start crying incessantly at twelve, the beginning of adolescence, suggests a grieving for innocence that captures the zeitgeist of the late 1960s. Prior to the turmoil of adolescence, Johnnas finds his artistic passion kindled by reading *The Negro Digest*, which under Hoyt W. Fuller's leadership, became, according to Clovis E. Semmes, "the most complete record of the Black Arts and Black Consciousness Movement" (196). His engagement with the influential journal is short-lived, however:

> The Negro Digest was prohibited in their house. Johnnas had become inflamed by the red print at the age of 10 and had set fire to an Irish friend who had neither ever read the Negro Digest

or really understood what it was that this culinary publication supplied to the Negro appetite that the Reader's Digest could not. Unfortunately, he almost learned that it was violence and a taste for his blood. (132)

In this irreverent, comical description, Johnnas's artistic development *almost* converges with a political consciousness shaped by a print vehicle for pan-African thought and original pieces related to Black Arts Movement (BAM) with an Afrocentric sensibility and political stance. The taste for his Irish friend's blood reckons with complex cultural history of race and white ethnic identity later captured by scholars such as Noel Ignatiev and his *How the Irish Became White*.

At his post–civil rights moment, Johnnas experiences the tension between opportunity and the thick residue of historical racism: "This open purse of American dreaming, though not intended for him, was, I must admit, not denied to him" (133). What does it mean to Johnnas to encounter the "open purse of American dreaming"? Is it a reference or critique related to capitalism, connected to commodification of aspirations, including artistic ones? His sensibility also becomes shaped by the "rags-to-riches" mythology, with references to his reading Horatio Alger under Hilly's tutelage: "He was a child thief and his mother was his accomplice. He had innocently ventured into the hazardous wilderness of his own unique being and here he would stay. He lost faith in his fellow human beings" (133). Hilly stands as an agent against collective identity, attempting to protect Johnnas's developing self from feeling any narrowing of possibility. Within the context of this *TDR* special issue, this emphasis on individual genius seems counterintuitive. However, she is mainly an "accomplice" in nurturing his liberation from expectations and limitations set within the context of white supremacy, particularly as it enters his education. She does not want parody and entertainment value for her son. She is nurturing an artist, and in *Johnnas*, the young artist faces humiliation and constraints from his peer group and his teachers.

Beyond his relationship with his mother, Johnnas encounters another potential mentor in his English teacher, who encourages his writing. Within this relationship, the price of integration for the gifted Black child becomes apparent, and the play raises a tension between the educational institutions, recalling the well-known words attributed to Malcom X that only fools allow their enemies to educate their children. Hilly is no fool, however, and she works to shape her son's consciousness to open and avoid restrictions. His writing reflects this freedom when, for example, he reads his "English story assignment" to his class and includes a part about wetting his bed and staining his sheets from the red dye in his Mickey Mouse doll's shorts, a child's organic lack of containment creating a new mark with cultural iconography.

This exchange between parent and teacher raises the issue of "giftedness," particularly as an educational designation and in relation to race. After his teacher encourages Johnnas, the child describes the creative emphasis provided within his home: "Oh, I write them on Sunday, my mother and I, we turn on the Sunday symphony and we write words together, it's a game, write the words the music makes you feel. It doesn't have to make sense, but then later we read it aloud and . . . sometimes it's very funny" (134). When the teacher tells Johnnas, "You mustn't stop writing," Johnnas replies, "No, I won't. My father and mother wouldn't let me" (134). The play emphasizes the artistic freedom and commitment stemming from a nurturing home life, while the institutions and peers attempt to restrict and confine Johnnas within narrow parameters of Blackness, such as when the neighborhood boys call him "toasty" or white-acting and "stuck up" (134). His mother stands as a lone ally against these restrictions, and in response to the pressure from his peers and his teacher, Hilly advocates for Johnnas's wholeness and uniqueness.

The teacher works one-on-one with Johnnas on his poetry but explains to him that he must complete his regular academic requirements to pass the course. The problem is in the way the teacher racialized Johnnas's giftedness, to which Hilly objects fiercely:

> I KNOW WHAT YOU TOLD HIM! . . . You tell my child that he is gifted . . . that he is special . . . that he has a terrible thing to fight in himself, what is this terrible thing? He comes to me and says, Mother, what is this terrible thing that my teacher talks about? Is it true? Because I am colored I am apt to be lazy and happy-go-lucky; it is a trait that Negroes are born with and adds to their charm, but in a writer, it is death? (135)

The teacher's mentorship remains compromised by his limited vision, the implicit bias that forms a blind spot to Johnnas's possibilities. The taxonomy associated with scientific racism that allowed Hill's twins to die untreated now enters the creative realm.

When the teacher maintains, "There are certain qualities ascribed to certain groups" (135), Hilly vehemently rejects this assault on the creative child she has nurtured since birth to belong to himself: "MY CHILD IS NOT A MEMBER OF ANY GROUP! He is not responsible to any group! I am responsible for him, and I tell him he is responsible now only to himself." What does Hilly's identification of Johnnas as an individual and her desire for him to be recognized as an individual mean in relation to this cultural moment? Hilly refuses to instill her child with a sense of limitations imposed by racism, and she confronts the teacher herself. Both plays have as a catalyst the confrontation with a teacher, who in some ways attempts to limit the horizons of the Black youth in their classrooms.

Hilly provides a witness throughout the play to Johnnas's uniqueness and reveals that Johnnas has a level of consciousness that surprises even her: "He's a good boy. He's such a kind boy. Already he shows such concern for things that in all my life I have never given a second thought." In her confrontation with the teacher, she tries to explain the ways she has struggled against the forces that would use his difference against him:

> I try to protect him, maybe too much, he has to become calloused out there on the streets to stand up against your groups. Suppose he passes all of your exams, what is going to become of him? Will it help him drown in a sea of respectability? I'm his mother and I already see in his face what his life will be if he lives, and I want him to know that it is not the end of the world if he does not desire to be black or white or yellow or green—my God, what do you want from him? . . . To replenish your supply of blacks. (136)

Johnnas is an interesting piece within the volume emphasizing a Black aesthetic and theater, a collective identity. The play engages several struggles at the same time, and perhaps Hilly's character as mother-witness articulates these struggles the most poignantly and forcefully. What does it mean to "drown in a sea of respectability"? Is that the life in which Hilly and Barney try to raise their child to shield him as much as possible from the world? What would it mean to breed an "individualist" in this context?

For Hilly, these questions remain tangled in the issues of assimilation within the school context, particularly as Johnnas becomes recognized as gifted. This recognition of his giftedness, rather than allowing him to soar and discover, places him "at risk" in a more insidious way. She demands that the teacher examine his motivations and his role:

> What do you think he needs you for? To integrate with? Why do you need him? To liberate? I liberated my son when I gave him life, and it killed me to see them waiting with their ready-made labels and their pigeon holes ready to stuff him in . . . race . . . Negro . . . When he was born his hair was the warmest color of brown; they wrote: hair black. His eyes were big, the color of new green; eyes brown, they wrote. (136)

In "Creativity and Equity: The Legacy of E. Paul Torrance as an Upstander for Gifted Black Males," T. C. Grantham notes, "During the 1950s when public schools were beginning to desegregate, gifted education expanded as a professional field and many segregationists strategically targeted gifted and advanced classes in newly desegregated schools to inappropriately continue a separate education for White students" (519). The teacher in *Johnnas* appears ready to engage his student's giftedness but unable to surpass the racialized limits set by previous models of mentorship. Hilly's previous experience has given her the gift of fear when considering the role white institutions of alleged care play in her children's lives. She demands proof that her surviving child will be recognized in his full humanity: "'Look at my child, look at him.' They never looked at him. Why can't you look at him? Why can't you listen to him? Suppose he goes mad someday; how will you help him?' (136). The teacher voices the implicit categorizations that limit the artistic development. In his absurd directness, he makes plain the way he remains entrenched in white supremacist idealogies: "It's just, Mrs. Gifford, that we feel that the child has a responsibility to society and society expects and needs the preservation of categories" (136). The teacher represents the absurdity and obscene logic of these limits, taxonomies, schemas when he responds: "Without blacks there would be no whites, without whites there would be blacks, and we're losing ground, we have to make room. We have placed millions of new seats in white restrooms all over the country now that the East Indians have been classified" (136).

Current discussions continue to raise the potential pitfalls when integrating Black children into white-majority, elite programs, such as Joe Brewster and Michèle Stephenson's 2014 documentary *American Promise*, reveal the cost for the children. In *American Promise*, two Black children, Seun and Idris, begin their education at Dalton, a prestigious Manhattan private school, together in kindergarten, and their families reveal their hopes for this opportunity and their child's social mobility. As the film progresses, difficulties emerge. At a particularly poignant moment, Idris is filmed talking to his parents: "A 9-year-old African-American boy lay on the couch, rubbing his head, and told his dad that if he just went to another school, life would be better. If he were just white, life would be better. He clarified, 'I'm not saying I want to . . . but isn't that right? That's what everyone else is saying'" (*American Promise*). His friend Seun faces problems inherent in what Soujourner's Jessica Breslin connects to "expectancy theory" when educators thwart his efforts to read more challenging books: "*They say you can't read something when you can . . . [T]hey say it's too hard for you . . . I get really frustrated*" (qtd. in Breslin). The parents-as-filmmakers hold the implicit bias and lowered expectations accountable in their documentary while also facing the way the parental desires influence the experience for their children.

In *Johnnas*, the white teacher introduces this assumption that the problem exists within Johnnas, that he must engage in an internal battle against his "nature," which would if allowed undermine his urge to produce and create. The teacher renders Blackness as a barrier to art, industriousness, creativity; in this message Blackness equals a kind of stasis. The irony is that the white teacher refers to perpetuation of certain static categories that impede creativity. The teacher-student relationship here echoes the ongoing problems experienced by Seun and Idris and the limitations placed on gifted Black students who face implicit bias barriers, even when identified as possessing special talents:

> Although there is increased focus on reducing the achievement gap between children of color and their peers who are white, many schools continue to deny African American students access to the very tools that could close this gap by denying them access to the gifted and talented programs. Moreover, African American students who do enter gifted and talented programs are more likely to drop out of these programs due to lack of mentorship and a feeling of isolation when they look for role models. (Moore and Neal 8)

Hilly recognizes the limitations of this mentorship and school as an engine of conformity. She has already faced impossible grief caused directly by Jim Crow and institutionalized racism. The death of her twins almost marked the end of her life as a mother. Hilly is trying to nurture a young Black artist and to counter the forces that would prevent her. This scene is one between a parent who recognizes the uniqueness of her own child with a representative of an institution that wants to mark him as ordinary and easy to control and shape. There has always been a sense that the artist does not do well in conventional environments such as schools. Hilly's encounter with the teacher here illuminates the struggle between a Black mother trying to get the world to *see* her child for who he is and not for his race only.

Even as Hilly fights to avoid this blurring or erasure of his individual features, she witnesses Johnnas coming to terms with the limits of the environment:

> He came to me that morning and said, "Mother, do people who don't have money who live in Philadelphia ever travel in Europe and Africa and maybe live there sometimes?" I said, "I've never known any who did." He looked at me a long time, then he looked away, sighed as though I had told him all there was to know. Then he walked away from the house. I never saw him again. (136)

Through his questioning, Johnnas confronts this sense that he may be trapped or have no immediate models for a more expansive life. This exchange leads to questions in interpreting playwright Gunn's choice to offer this perspective from the point of view of a child. In this move, the child as a figure of hope that reaches beyond what had previously existed is challenged when Johnnas appears to accept his mother's answer as a final judgment. What is also notable in this moment is that Johnnas reaches out for both Africa and Europe. This could signal a desire for a sense of the merging of cultures in the current American art forms or it

The Problematic of the Young, Gifted, and Black Artist in *Johnnas*   41

could reflect his desire to find others who sought lineage, origins, influence. No one's ever traveling may also suggest a kind of stagnation within the current state. Johnnas looks to his mother for an escape route to a place that does not attempt to limit him into categories or expectations of small proportions. When she cannot offer him that possibility, he walks into the world without a sense of horizon.

Barney reflects about Johnnas's attempt to share his vision and sensibility when he arranges for his friend Hank to escort Johnnas's friend and muse Loretta to a dance. Loretta, a dark-skinned Black girl, is summarily rejected by Hank, who is so offended that Johnnas would have him be seen in public with Loretta that he assaults Johnnas when he next sees him (137)

Barney recounts, "They said Hank stood over him and was yellin' things like, you punk, mother-fucker, you make me go out with a black nappy-haired bitch like that Loretta. You told me she was beautiful, with pretty hair. I'll beat your ass, embarrass me with that black ass chick" (137). In this moment, Johnnas stands as a young artist who embraces Loretta as a beauty ideal, as a living expression of the political "Black is beautiful" mantra. By choosing Loretta as an ideal, Johnnas appears to transcend the indirect, white-mediated avenues to artistic freedom and expression: parody and the spectacle of songs, vaudeville, and cakewalk. Their relationship offers honesty and critique in a way that reflects their lives as midcentury Black children. She alerts him when he needs to code-switch, referring to "ofay" "grey boys," when he dances and that the other girls laugh (117). She tries to encourage him and give him tips on how to impress girls and embody a more appealing masculinity that did not suggest "whiteness." In this relationship, he learns the "dance" between and within perceived authenticity and identity as a youth and as an artist developing in his public persona. However, the subsequent rejection from peers places him in a precarious existential space, particularly in the profoundly painful encounter, Johnnas faces the internalized racism of his friend through the disparagement of Loretta. His suicide scene is narrated by his mother. A crowd cheers him on as he stands on a building ledge and then jumps. The scene following his suicide includes his dancing with Loretta. In this scene, Loretta points out all Johnnas's inadequacies. He acts young, appears effeminate, but he knows Loretta is his friend. She reassures him that "they're just jealous" (137). He continues to receive messages that he is wrong for this world. Hilly responds to Johnnas's sense of alienation: "I don't care, that was my boy . . . I didn't understand him. He was deep alright. That don't mean shit to me, cause he was mine, you hear me? . . . He was mine." For Hilly, Johnnas had not had enough opportunity to embrace the full meaning of his relation to art as a life-source: "Why? . . . all that writing things down all the time, livin' in the movies, sittin' around . . . if we had talked . . . if I had told him that I've never liked it here either. If I had told him that it was always gonna be for him everything . . ." (138). Through her maternal grief, she identifies a crisis in the radical estrangement marking the Black artist's struggle to reach full potential as embodied by her beloved son.

The play ends with Barney and Hilly listening intently to Johnnas as he shares the pages filled with his imagination. "Fumbling over a pile of papers he had stuck carelessly between the covers of his loose-leaf notebook," they find a poem that concludes: "Nothing in the pockets of our old coats can save us now" (138), which leaves the audience with the question about what can save or restore. What kind of artist is required at this point in time? In *Johnnas*, the outside world threatens the young artist's development and, in the end, his very life. It has long been a part of the mythology around the creatively gifted that they have heightened sensitivity and feel out of touch with the real world. What does it really mean to be young, gifted, and Black in Johnnas's experience?

Gunn appears to place the blame for Johnnas's rejection and pain in the outside world. His family unit is nurturing, and Barney, while he admits to his inability to understand Johnnas completely, accepts and is willing to bear full witness to Johnnas's growth as an artist. In the years shortly after Johnnas's flight, Nina Simone released "Young, Gifted, and Black" and sang her ode to the Johnnas children of this world, including a visit to the stoops of Sesame Street on February, 1972, the same year that the federal government defined gifted students (Moore and Neal 4). A. S. Sloan considers the song and the range of its vision:

> When Nina Simone and Weldon Irvine, Jr. wrote the song, "To Be Young, Gifted, and Black," I wonder if they had any idea what kind of monsters they were spawning. I don't mean this derogatorily. That sweet, earnest song created in honor of the playwright and activist Lorraine Hansberry garnered a spirit of love and support for generations of black children to come, but it also opened up the possibility for the kind of offspring that could defy, embarrass, and dishonor the best intentions of their creators. They will be young, gifted for sure, and in some way or another black (or, as LaValle calls Obama, "blackish"). But will their gifts match the sweet hopes, aesthetic tendencies, and social vision of the elders who made their privilege possible? Absolutely not. Who even knew that a black sci-fi nerd was possible in 1970? (979)

It is not clear—based on the way that Johnnas as an adult/writer frames the narration—whether the "jump" is the leap into freedom and the unknown. Was it a "suicide" of a self that allowed external forces to define him and his creativity? The child who can be mentored and who has to counter the limitations of bullies (who are encaged) and the teacher—and the parents who, while nurturing are also stifling because of their own posttraumatic response and risk aversion. In the plays' final moments, Johnnas's parents remain actively listening to his poem, his words:

"The dissolving of crystals— / the nets break / letting serpents of the sea at our boats— / the call is on, / and the roll of the distant drum / heralds the on-crush of time." Johnnas conjures images of endings and the need for new tools or resources: "The childhood beetles are dead, / the penknife rusted, / the top has lost its string / and will not spin" (138). There is something Blakean—"And what rough beast, its hour come round at last, / Slouches towards Bethlehem to be born?"—in this poem, and it suggests the necessity for shedding skins, or as James T. Stewart puts it in "The Development of the Black Revolutionary Artist": "We are, in essence, the ingredients that will create the future. For this reason, we are misfits, estranged from the white cultural present. Historically and sociologically, we are the rejected. Therefore, we must know that we are building stories for a New Era. In our movement toward the future, 'ineptitude' and 'unfitness' will be an aspect of what we do" (6). If the old coats and childhood items become useless, then as Peter Labrie indicates in "The New Breed": "New folkways, new moves are being developed. But before they become structured, the old ones must be vomited up. This means a process of shock, disruption, and transformation. It can be a violent and frightening process . . . [and also] there is a deeper, more creative and constructive aspect to it" (75). Perhaps this process includes a gesture so unsettling as Bill Gunn's representation of a young Black artist's suicide in *Johnnas* to signal the problematic his being embodies and the relevant yet unresolved questions around integregation, inspiration, and liberation for the young, gifted, and Black.

CHAPTER 2

"MY PORTRAIT IS GOLD"

Resiliency and the Crisis of the Black Child's Image in Dael Orlandersmith's *The Gimmick*

People who don't invent themselves, who are so bitter, so blinded, who cease to question, have made peace with defeat.
—James Baldwin

At a critical moment in Dael Orlandersmith's solo performance piece *The Gimmick*, which premiered in 1998 at Princeton's McCarter Theatre and New Haven's Long Wharf Theatre, two African American young people reunite in a painful exchange. Jimmy is a teen painter who has been "discovered" by the predominately white downtown art scene and who has now abandoned his friend Alexis, a nascent writer. They have had a mutually nurturing relationship since they met in 1968 and found their way into creativity in the Harlem documented by Gordon Parks's 1967 photo essay "A Harlem Family," featured in the *Life* magazine issue: "The Cycle of Despair: The Negro and the City." At the beginning of a post–civil rights era, with Black urban life at the center of public debate and de facto segregation caused by white flight to the suburbs, cities burned in response to state-sanctioned violence and neglect. In this critical moment, Jimmy betrays this bond when he asks Alexis to return his nude portrait of her, one that celebrates their intimacy and the dreams of a creative life beyond the Gimmick or hustle of the Harlem streets. It also depicts her body in a positive, loving fashion. Jimmy sells her portrait for drug money.

Jimmy's life and death raise significant questions about what it means to be young, gifted, and Black in Harlem and to succumb to addiction in the late 1960s and 1970s, when dreams remained deferred in desperate material conditions and traumatic legacies, and this chapter focuses on what the crisis between Jimmy and Alexis signals, particularly about the relationship between image and word in shared memory and the struggle to sustain a collaborative creative life that resists the pull of Gimmicks in their various undermining forms, including addiction to substances that both numb and destroy.

Similar to Johnnas in the previous chapter, Jimmy, as a young artist developing his aesthetic sensibilities, finds a muse in a young Black female friend. While Loretta is rejected by one of Johnnas's peers, Alexis's image is embraced and commodified by the white art world, which results in a kind of betrayal of the young people's bond as friends and artists. This betrayal scene serves as a site of inquiry for the distress it evokes within Alexis and in their friendship. Although their friendship began to unravel earlier as Jimmy seemed to favor a "Modigliani" white girl from the downtown art scene to Alexis's "Picasso" fullness, this final loss associated with the nude image causes Alexis to spin into a full-blown crisis. Reacting to the surrender of her portrait, Alexis finds Jimmy and follows him into a local drug den, where she succumbs to the "Stuff n' Gimmicks," or "the scratch n' nod" of lesser dreams, claiming that she will give up her words and colors to maintain a connection with her lost friend. When she is high, Jimmy's addict father Clarence rapes her. After the attack, she returns home, and her mother wants to bring her to church for God to cleanse her. Watching her mother cry "vodka tears," Alexis has lost faith. She then desires to self-harm. In this poignant moment, we see Alexis abandon herself. She externalizes the sense of abandonment she feels not only from Jimmy, but also from her entire world. Her dreams of escaping the blight have been based on a shared creative venture, but Jimmy and Alexis do not share this escape. Jimmy's quick rise to fame and his urge to remove himself from his painful history has led him to addiction and ultimately to early death.

For Orlandersmith, *The Gimmick* explores the differences in outcomes for young people facing similar precarity, and she describes her inspiration in an interview for *American Theatre*:

> Peter Askin, whom I'd worked with on several earlier projects, came up with the idea. We started talking about the world of children, the dreams of children. He asked something about how kids from similar backgrounds, similarly difficult environments, fare so differently—how some children who are so spirited and seem like they have what it takes to beat the odds, don't end up beating the odds, while others make it out. I said, "Let me see if *I* can come up with the story." (Coleman)

In *The Gimmick*, the shared story of Alexis and Jimmy splits apart, and the crisis around the lost image serves as an irreparable break in the friendship. The painting's exchange appears provocative because it gestures toward a profound loss: a creative young Black woman has lost control of an image of herself. This image depicts her naked and vulnerable, looking at loving eyes that capture her in this moment, returning the intimacy and knowledge. The loss of the image sparks an intense response that urges a consideration of the larger cultural treatment of Black women and girls' vulnerability combined with the risks required for creative life. There are at least two levels at which this crisis operates. The loss of the painting marks the end of a creative partnership essential for her growth and also invokes a traumatic collective memory related to the circulation of images of Blackness and vulnerability in the larger public sphere.

According to Jeffrey C. Alexander, "cultural trauma occurs when members of a collectivity feel they have been subjected to a horrendous event that leaves indelible marks upon their group consciousness" (1), and with this meaning in mind, is it possible to read Alexis's crisis in symbolic relation to other "horrendous events" involving a Black child or youth and including the circulation of the child's image in the public sphere? *The Gimmick* suggests the complexity involved when considering the explicit Black adolescent body in the visual realm both as a legacy and a cultural phenomenon that recurs in the time of the play's initial production. A rupture occurs between Jimmy's visual and Alexis's literary realms, which reinforces associations of hypervisibility without an accompanying intimately-connected narrative for the Black adolescent body in public space.

Similar to the *TDR* special issue that includes *Johnnas*, *The Gimmick* begins in 1968: "It's 1968 . . . and the Black panthers and the young lords, them/they scream, 'pick up the gun'" (79). The play's title factors significantly in relation to the culture or scene, and "The Gimmick" that informs the lives of the young artists is linked to late 1960s Harlem, shortly after the major gains of the civil rights era. By 1968, considerable public focus had shifted from the earlier southern civil rights movement to the unrest in urban centers such as Detroit, Watts, and New York City's Harlem. Assembled in response to the uprisings in cities such as Detroit, Newark, Watts, and Chicago, the Kerner Commission report released in 1968 summarizes the causes of the distress: "This is our basic conclusion: Our nation is moving toward two societies, one Black, one white—separate and unequal." The report identifies the interconnectedness and complicity of the white majority in creating the crisis that led to the uprisings:

> Violence and destruction must be ended—in the streets of the ghetto and in the lives of people. Segregation and poverty have created in the racial ghetto a destructive environment totally

unknown to most white Americans. What white Americans have never fully understood but what the Negro can never forget—is that white society is deeply implicated in the ghetto. White institutions created it, white institutions maintain it, and white society condones it.

In addition to the culpability of mainstream societal institutions, through mainstream news outlets, images of Black youth, reacting with despair-fueled rage at unrelenting neglect and brutality, circulated widely, further exacerbating the negative effects. The Kerner report became one of several commissions investigating the unrest, and each report seemed to align itself with the spirit of varying political partisanship, creating competing narratives for public consumption:

> The 1965–1970 trauma of nationwide carnage resulted in riot commission blame, with the McCone Commission taking a hard-line conservative view of riffraff rioting, the Kerner Commission countering with a liberal indictment of deeply rooted American racism, the Violence Commission leaning cautiously back toward the moderate right, and the Scranton Commission somewhat surprisingly leaning left again. (Graham 8)

These commission responses correspond to the rising concern about urban life as a "study" or "social problem" with "at risk" youth in the center of the controversy with their images circulating widely in media sources that may not have always fleshed out the narratives of their lived experiences as individuals. Instead, the youth find themselves in one-dimensional, "menace-to-society" representations, susceptible to the flattening that occurs during moral panics and in need of extreme measures to contain their expressions of pain. This scene repeats itself in contemporary America as we witness, for example, Black mothers celebrated for physically removing teenage boys from the protests in Baltimore following Freddie Gray's killing at police hands while obscuring the motivation behind their outrage. In this scenario, the public response requires a closer look to reveal the underlying bias against Black teens, such as provided by scholar-journalist Stacey Patton:

> Praising [Toya] Graham distracts from a hard truth: It doesn't matter how Black children behave—whether they throw rocks at the police, burn a CVS, join gangs, walk home from the store with candy in their pocket, listen to rap music in a car with friends, play with a toy gun in a park, or simply make eye contact with a police officer—they risk being killed and blamed for their own deaths because Black youths are rarely viewed as innocent or worthy of protection.

This response becomes a deflection from systemic issues, and as Patton concludes: "The message becomes: Black children's behavior is the true enemy of peace."

Set within this fraught landscape at an earlier historical point, when urban youth of color also faced their stories told by removed and often hostile sources, *The Gimmick* centers around another creatively gifted Black young person, Alexis, a burgeoning writer who narrates her confrontation with a despair that threatens to undermine her sense of possibility. Alexis and her friend Jimmy begin the journey toward an edifying creative life together, and Jimmy's surrender to internal and external demons threatens Alexis's ability to claim her gifts. In *The Gimmick*, scenes of innocence and experience merge, thus depicting the harsher aspects of Harlem life for young people without diminishing their youthful perspectives, such as when the two children get ice cream from the Mr. Softie truck and begin discussing whether "Tootsie's a hoe" (81). They engage in a conversation about the definition and characters of "hoes" and how Alexis should avoid becoming one after Jimmy reveals that his "pops says all women are hoes" (81). Jimmy wants Alexis to stay away from men, so she can circumvent the "hoe" label, indicating an internal association with purity and the freedom they share together as young people beyond the reach of "Gimmicks." Together they embody "youthful sweetness / we're excited by this / licking our ice cream cones we could have been kids anywhere / we were kids anywhere / the sweetness meant good / the sweetness meant underneath we wanted goodness" (81). This ode to innocence continues, with its repetition serving as emphasis and incantation: "We're reaching for goodness / we're reaching for the sweetness of childhood / the sweetness meant no Gimmicks / no hustle / we the kids in Harlem / were sweet / it was there / it is there / the hope / the sweetness / There was / is a Beauty in Harlem" (81). The "Beauty" stands in contrast with the "Gimmicks." Gimmicks disrupt childhood innocence and dehumanize adults. In their innocence, they also connect to a more universal experience of childhood, with the specific context close yet unable to permeate the boundaries they share: "Beyond Gimmicks and Hustles / Next to Gimmicks / Hustles / there is a Beauty / back then me and Jimmy had hope" (82). Alexis, who dreams of the writer's life, finds sustenance when she recognizes that her dreams remain valid when her world restricts her growth. The "rose from concrete" referenced in the chapter's opening is a familiar metaphor for the genius that arises from late-twentieth-century urban blight. The rose here suggests a manifestation of creation, something organic and seemingly fragile breaking through reified barriers. Beauty includes the hardness from which it emerges. A rose in concrete has an unexpected beauty, which contains a divergent thinking, a shocking contrast, a dissonance without which metaphor, the essence of poetry, cannot exist.

 Jimmy and Alexis are creative spirits, a new generation that can promise the community a new hope. They generate meaning in their cultural expression, which bears witness to the life they see around them. They must balance reality and dreams against the "Gimmicks," or hustles that allow escape from reality but undermine their dreamers ultimately. In "The New Breed," an essay published in *The Negro Digest* during the same period, Peter Labrie identifies the particular changes in the context that shape a new generation's perspective:

> The Black world has changed so dramatically since before and after World War II that it would be impossible for a youth coming up today to have the same view of the world himself as his father had. In the turbulent, lawless cities of America, the rhythm of life is quicker and more varied and complex for the masses. Life has become a game in which one has to learn at an early age to be flexible, to scheme and hustle if he is to survive. (71)

Alexis and Jimmy witness the "Gimmick" or hustle but establish a world beyond its reach with each other through their creative connections. Their relationship provides a contrast between the illusion of freedom found in the Gimmick, which mainly thrives on escapism through drugs and easy money. The "Gimmick" requires participation with transitory, fleeting "highs" that contrast in the play with the sustenance found in creative culture. By witnessing the adults surrounding them, the two young artists can see addiction as a symptom and temporary management of trauma that in turn leads to more exposure to trauma. The freedom essential for risk-taking to generate new perspectives is in tension with post-traumatic experience but essential for artmaking. Through their relationship, they mitigate risk-aversion, and together, Alexis and Jimmy stand in a liberating vulnerability and trust as they embrace their artistic passions, even as Alexis reflects, "We were always old . . . [S]till we got older and more guarded" (83) toward outside interference.

Alexis notes that the transition between childhood and into the stage of adolescence requires particular vigilance against the lure of "Gimmicks." Jimmy's early self-protection strategies include inventing a Superman character who fights drug dealers (76), and the children escape in their fantasies using American Bandstand as well. Jimmy's father disrupts the fantasy, calling it "whitey shit" and closing off the possible identification with the blue ocean landscape and dancing: "That's got nothing to do wichy'all" (78). And in this exchange, after deriding them for their hope, he sexualizes Alexis, who at the time is likely around ten (she is eight when they meet and fourteen at the next time her age is noted), foreshadowing his predatory nature toward Alexis. The play relies in many ways on stock characters of adult zombies, the walking dead addicts who, in the legacy of poverty and disenfranchisement, appear to exist outside a moral code beyond the Gimmick.

Defined through several images throughout the play, Gimmicks always seem to lead back to a sense of impotence to change circumstances and the ways this hopelessness manifests when directed inward and toward community: "The Gimmick is also / looking at the cracks in your wall you call home / realizing it's a ghetto / wanting to leave it but not having the courage" (83), and "The Gimmick is blood / a blood circus / how much blood can pour onto the streets of Harlem / on our block in Harlem" (83). Gimmicks appear as trickster figures or behaviors existing outside of mainstream culture, but instead of offering resistance or covert undermining of oppressive norms, they seduce and undermine the disenfranchised community. Significantly, the Gimmick hinders artistic development since it does not allow for challenge, change, or agency: "The Gimmick is not reinventing yourself / thinking someone owes you something / the Gimmick is being down, so low, low to the Ground not knowing / realizing you have a choice / or maybe you do realize you have a choice / and you care and leave / or don't care at all and stay / don't care and you shoot it / cut it / stomp it / scream it" (83). The Gimmick speaks to the despair existing within what Maysa Akbar defines as "Urban Trauma":

> Within Urban Trauma, to be in despair means that you do not care about much: not about yourself, others, community, or even

survival. You have completely given up and are simply existing, certainly not living. Despair at this level may involve passive suicidal thoughts, with associated considerations of what it would feel like to end it all. There is a level of desperation and impatience that accompanies this level of despair—a general feeling of being stuck in life, with no clear indication of how to purposefully move out of your current situation and into a more productive place. The combination of not caring and feeling stuck will sometimes lead people in despair to make irrational and impulsive decisions without thinking through the consequences. Despair in Urban Trauma does not consider life in milestones, instead life in general is considered an unbeatable struggle and obstacles seem insurmountable, the weight of which is intolerable to carry. (134)

The play most often associates Gimmicks with addictions as well as associated ways to deflect from facing reality directly. The Gimmicks exacerbate the estrangement within family caused by despair and the desire to find relief from overwhelming conditions.

Escape comes in many forms, and the pervasive drug use contrasts with the potentially productive fantasy life that allows Alexis and Jimmy to dream about a creative life in Paris. For Alexis, "I close my eyes and let the words help get me to places" (84). Like Johnnas, the characters create travel fantasies or suggest interest in traveling beyond their home context, and they transport toward freedom through the imaginary realm: "A Harlem Black boy and a Harlem Black girl and 'California Dreamin's' got nothin to do with us' / Me and Jimmy are ten and twelve or maybe eleven and thirteen, we're walking / walking Downtown / walking together" (86). At a time when the cultural/Black Power/Black Arts emphasis is on moving away from Eurocentric aesthetic influences, the children look to Europe, particularly France, as an escape and artistic sanctuary, mainly in a gesture toward James Baldwin (and Nina Simone and Richard Wright). Art stands in contrast to the Gimmick as creativity and addiction appear in contrast and relation throughout the play, and both share a connection to the lived experience of the neighborhood. When an argument between an addicted couple disrupts the librarian's first conversation with Alexis, Miss Innis quotes Baldwin: "'People who don't invent themselves / who are so bitter / so blinded / who cease to question / have made peace with defeat'" (850). Sources of creativity also exist as catalysts for addictive behavior, and this negotiation tests the capacity of these two developing artists.

The Gimmick stages the continual tension between flights of fantasy that allow the artist to feel empowered to take risks and break away from conventions or expectations that make stifle growth and the essential need to have an archive, repository, community on which to draw inspiration through synthesis and divergence with artistic legacies. The one person who consistently nurtures her growth does so by reinforcing consistently this validity. The sustenance provided by the librarian, Ms. Innis, involves simple but powerful reminders that Alexis has a gift and a dream to realize it. From the beginning of their relationship, Miss Innis serves as a conduit to artistic legacies who also allows Alexis to feel seen, albeit uncomfortably at first: "The lady that works there / stares at me . . . The lady just stares / stares" (84). This staring causes Alexis to worry that she had done something wrong, and Alexis responds guardedly to the librarian's initial approach. Later when she realizes that Miss Innis recognizes her as a lover of words, being seen no longer comes with a sense of dread and threat in the space of the library. She introduces Alexis to James Baldwin, who "used words to carry him off the streets of Harlem" (85). As she hands Alexis *Another Country*, Miss Innis repeats the word "waste" as a caution, validating and warning Alexis about her potential through a sustained relationship with writing.

Jimmy too finds a mentor for his development as an artist in Mr. Kauffman, who provides him with studio space and materials and who introduces him to the downtown art scene. This introduction to the downtown arts scene raises a critique of neoliberalism's focus on individual escape through talent and market forces alone. Echoing Baldwin's words from the previous chapter on the critical importance of community for Black artists and the political-aesthetic considerations presented in the *TDR* issue on Black theater, *The Gimmick* raises questions about the risks involved when the Black artist separates from the context of community. Although Jimmy sees the possibility of life beyond the Gimmicks of ghetto life with its poverty, addiction, the violence connected to disenfranchisement, his connections and comparisons to Picasso suggest both his desire to transcend the particulars of identity and the problems arising from alignment with Picasso. If this is a survival story and a cautionary tale, we witness Jimmy seek validation outside the Black community, and his success is fleeting. He survives in Alexis's story. At that moment, the resiliency of the African American Women's literary movement is clarified through the young, gifted, Black woman writer who survives the vulnerability of Black girlhood and the broken promises of the Gimmick through her relationship with Miss Innis, the librarian who stands in for the archive, the history, the legacy. Like Baldwin's words about his sweet Lorraine, sweet, strong Alexis survives by placing her art in relation to both her dreams of Paris and the earth of Mount Morris Park, a walk away from the library.

While James Baldwin is Alexis's inspiration and role model—and it seems particularly important that he hails from Harlem as well—Jimmy finds himself drawn to Picasso. Although Orlandersmith's characters often find cross-cultural creative influences, it may be relevant that Jimmy's role model exists outside any connection to his experience. Unlike James Baldwin, Alexis's inspirational figure, Picasso, does not offer a bridge from the estrangement felt by the young Black artist. He does not share an experience with Jimmy the way that Alexis finds with Baldwin. Baldwin models the risks that come from liberation and continues to express the ongoing process, reflecting the existential aspects of being a Black artist in America.

Jimmy's story suggests that visual art presents additional challenges, particularly involving access to resources. The visual arts appear much less accessible and inclusive historically. The complex relationship between Blackness and in/visibility politics influences the visual artist's journey. Writer bell hooks describes the deep impression left by her relationship with a painter as a young person:

> Life taught me that being an artist was dangerous. The one grown Black person I met who made art lived in a Chicago basement. A distant relative of my father's, cousin Schuyler was talked about as someone who had wasted his life dreaming about art. He was lonely, sad, and broke. At least that was how folks saw him. I do not know how he saw himself, only that he loved art. (1)

As hooks notes, community understanding becomes challenging when the artist appears to exacerbate the financial precarity resulting from structural racism with the choice to live as an artist. This isolation would seem to make the artist more vulnerable to the exploitation of market forces.

In *Knocking the Hustle: Against the Neoliberal Turn in Black Politics*, Lester Spence discusses the "neoliberal turn, the gradual embrace of the general idea that society (and every institution within it) works best when it works according to the principles of the market," which pervades collective life. Spence identifies the historical period in which *The Gimmick* is set as the point at which the "neoliberal turn" begins to take hold:

> For a variety of reasons we've been forced to hustle and grind our way out of the post–civil rights era, and it is this hustle and grind in all of its institutional manifestations that's resulted in our current condition. . . . The hustle. The concept of the "hustler" has changed somewhat over the past thirty years or so. Whereas in the late sixties and early seventies the hustler was someone who consistently sought to get over, the person who tried to do as little work as possible in

order to make ends meet, with the "hustled" being the people who were victimized by these individuals ("He hustled me"), the hustler is now someone who consistently works. (Foreword)

Jimmy's involvement in both the downtown art scene, where his identity as a young artist becomes shaped by market forces that make comparisons and demands based on consumer desire, and the pervasive influence of Tootsie's underground economy, interferes with his creative development rather than providing freedom. However, the play does not linger in its attention to the downtown art scene and its propensity to corrupt but focuses mainly on Jimmy's resulting fragility when removed from Alexis and the connection she provides.

The Gimmick does not offer a cautionary tale about hubris and art and complicates the notion that opportunity alone allows for untethered upward mobility. The Mr. Kauffmans and Genevieves of the world are not directly responsible for Jimmy's downfall but are connected to it through their "innocence" or obliviousness to Jimmy's inner struggles. They offer opportunity and generosity without a sense of the unresolved emotions that Jimmy must navigate and the ways that has internalized the Gimmicks he has encountered since childhood.

A core truth haunts Jimmy's journey: no art can be created in a vacuum, and originality entails making new from the existing materials. For Jimmy, the materials he draws from require a resilience to evoke and manage the emotional upheaval that may accompany such an evocation. This resilience requires the bond that is disrupted when the creative expression between intimates leaves African American geographical space of Harlem and becomes commodified in the predominantly white downtown art establishment. It is not the movement that places the artist at risk, but the break from feeling truly seen and known. Throughout *The Gimmick*, Alexis finds strength in James Baldwin and his move to Paris, so here we turn to him for perspective on the Black creative experience in the second half of the twentieth century United States. To return to Baldwin's words from his foreword essay "Sweet Lorraine," James Baldwin introduces Lorraine Hansberry's *To Be Young, Gifted, and Black* with tribute to his late friend, and in this tribute, he describes Hansberry's struggles with finding an artistic home in twentieth-century America as a Black woman. For Baldwin, the artist must remain connected to community: "To continue to grow, to remain in touch with himself, he needs the support of that community from which, however, all of the pressures of American life incessantly conspire to remove him. And when he is effectively removed, he falls silent—and the people have lost another hope" (xviii). In *The Gimmick*, this search for an enriching connection to community is complicated by Gimmicks at home and isolation when away from home.

The Gimmick and Baldwin raise the question: If the rose and its block of concrete were cut and placed under glass for audiences to speculate upon and observe, what would happen? Where are the rose's roots? According to bell hooks:

> Current commodification of Blackness may mean that the white folks who walk through exhibits of works by such artists as Bettye and Alison Saar are able to be more in touch with this work than most Black folks. These circumstances will change only as African Americans and our allies renew the progressive Black liberation struggle—reenvisioning Black revolution in such a way that we create collective awareness of the radical place that art occupies within the freedom struggle and the way in which experiencing art can enhance our understanding of what it means to live as free subjects in an unfree world. (9)

In contrast with the fleeting happiness aligned with "market" access, Alexis's relationship with writing brings us to a space grounded within community. The library represents an archival or collective memory site that offers respite from the external struggles by accessing an internal legacy. The library is the connection to writers who have gone before and thrived within their work. It is an incubator for the young Black artist to reflect within herself rather than reproduce an image of herself for outside circulation.

Jimmy's initial work suggests a proto-hip hop aesthetics that depicts the subjectivity within the dehumanizing landscape of urban abandonment and decline of the late twentieth century. Jimmy's inner struggle is similar to the way rapper Vic Mensa describes his own battle with addiction and mental health issues while trying to evolve as a young artist of color based in Chicago: "The voices in my head keep talking . . . / 'You'll never be good enough . . . you never was / . . . You hurt everyone around you, you're impossible to love / . . . I wish you were never born, we would all be better for it / . . . You're still a drug addict, you're nothing without your medicine / Go and run to your sedative, you can't run forever, Vic'" (qtd. in Brown). Mensa's honest grappling with his issues received considerable attention after his autobiographical album's release: "Mensa's 'The Autobiography' was a landmark in this conversation last year. The album is unsparing about his own descent into addiction but wise and empathetic about the causes of dependency (among them, the violence, isolation, and hopelessness in poor minority communities) and the possibility of redemption" (Brown). Resourced initially from available materials, repurposed to create a sustainable, living beat, artistic forms such as hip hop enter the mainstream markets that cultivate an appetite for expressions of Black pain while the artist's inner struggle goes unnoticed.

In their special issue on Black masculinity, "Introduction Black Masculinities and the Matter of Vulnerability," Darius Bost, La Marr Jurelle Bruce, and Brandon J. Manning indicate that their work "also draws attention to dangers rarely highlighted in public discourse about Black masculine vulnerability: childhood trauma, sexual violence, loneliness, depression, indignity, and self-loathing, among others. We believe that any critical engagement with Black masculinity and vulnerability must attend to the interior lives of Black masculine subjects and grapple with intimate, invisible, and quiet forms of violence" (1). In expressing his sense of estrangement, Jimmy demonstrates a desire for liberation that seems essential to his art. It is an opportunity, but like all other opportunities to cross racial boundaries or previously segregated spaces—the ultimate cost is felt by the Black young person. The gift cannot be separated from the lived experience of the artist here. How would Jimmy's new companions deal with the complex range of his emotional register? What was their relationship to Blackness? It is not enough to appreciate and admire the performance. They may not have been undermining in the same way as the teacher in *Johnnas* in that the play provides no textual evidence that viewed Jimmy as limited due to race. However, there is no sense that he is more than a novelty or an "opportunity" to "lift up" a young Black artist. He is a "discovery" who is too young to have even discovered himself and the legacy of the painful Gimmick to which he had been exposed regularly. The pain of the familiar is preferred to the pain of the unknown, and the rise came with complications and disruptions that the surface striving and ambition (as priorities) does not acknowledge.

Jimmy takes a great risk when he exposes himself to the outside world and allows Mr. Kauffman to bring his art to the downtown galleries. For Jimmy, it seems that this vulnerability results in accolades, but the success does not eradicate the pain of parental rejection. Instead, the attention highlights the original wound. In his success, Jimmy finds himself removed from connections to his community. His father, Clarence, has always reacted with disdain to Jimmy's painting, and then when he fights with Alexis, he finds himself without a connection to his family, community, or history.

When Jimmy begins working in Mr. Kaufman's studio, he "paints angry pieces / frightened boys / frightened Black girls / crying Black boys / crying Black girls" (90). Alexis describes his painting called *Solo* depicting a young boy looking through the locked bars of his Harlem window, an image similar to the young Fontenelle sons from Gordon Parks's *Life* magazine piece. "It was the color spectrum of pain," Alexis recalls, "pain in total color / slashes of light / color / Jimmy knew it from Clarence / I knew it from Lenny. / How each slap / punch / was a spectrum of orange red Black blue" (90). Alexis has had enough of this pain and pleads with to paint from love, to paint life, to paint her:

> One day I said to Jimmy, "Let's make the colors happy colors / not just hurt colors / let's make them happy." Jimmy frowns / frowns some more "what do you mean, Alexis?" / I say, "Not just orange-red blood, Jimmy. Think of something good with orange-red" / Jimmy says, "I can only think of blood, Alexis" / "But blood keeps you alive, Jimmy / Think about it keeping you alive / Like when we go to Paris / blood keeps you alive" / Jimmy grins / grins some more / "Red, orange blood is life / not just pain / it's life" / And I say, "Yeah, Jimmy / life." (90)

In this scene, Alexis mediates Jimmy's experience as he perceives reality and his medium of artist expression. To alter a visual artist's relationship to color seems profound and an indication of the depth of their mutual connection. For Jimmy, it is also a foreshadowing moment of his impressionability, his innocence, and his dependency. Alexis would not accept his artistic vision as an expression of violence. He seemed to remain trapped in negativity. Alexis suggests an orientation toward "Paris," the escape that allows hope to remain. Jimmy's initial expression related to traumatic memory or posttraumatic experience appears to Alexis to be "stuck" in the repetition of the most painful depictions, but perhaps it is arguable as to whether that instinct to move into more positive thinking at that moment was ultimately to Jimmy's benefit. Did Jimmy need this outlet, this way to externalize his pain and to make it visible? In the relationship between the artist-subject and the Black youth pain he brought to the surface through visual art, there was a space of recognition not often allowed in a world that denies Black pain. Through Jimmy's early paintings, he shows a complexity of representation and the connection between the artist's emotional landscape and the chosen subjects. According to artist Charles White, "Art must be an integral part of the struggle. It can't simply mirror what's taking place. It must adapt itself to human needs. It must ally itself with the forces of liberation. . . . I have no use for artists who try to divorce themselves from the struggle" (Elliot and White 828). For Jimmy, representing the struggle focuses on a personal level. His art releases the pain experienced by young people in impossible circumstances, but a risk accompanies this vulnerability as Maysa Akbar notes:

> Vulnerability is the antithesis of living in Urban Trauma. Becoming vulnerable means you open yourself up to losing at this game called life. Building a wall to protect your heart, your emotions, and deter anything from hurting you again becomes one of the primary tenets of survival. I, like many others, have learned my way around survival. By now I would most certainly have a doctorate in Survival Tactics if there was one granted by the School of Hard Knocks. Learning your way around survival isolates you. It is hard to consider others in your circle, even those who want to help, or do right by you, because you don't trust; in fact, you cannot trust. Trusting in people is a violation, just as much as vulnerability. Eventually you adapt to living this way. (138)

The vulnerability also suggests a larger risk in circulating images of Black adolescent pain and the history this circulation conjures. Similar to hip hop's exposure to commodification and co-option, Jimmy's painting releases images of Black youth suffering into a white downtown art scene, with the accompanying anxiety that these images would reinforce stereotypes about Black life.

The images also navigate the historical associations with the explicit Black body, particularly in suffering or violation, as a visual spectacle. According to Leigh Raiford, "photographs of lynching embody the will to survive and the anguish of failure entrenched in critical Black memory. Photography has been central to the narration of lynching across the twentieth century, and lynching photography is nearly omnipresent in the narration of Black life in this long century as well" (120). In the second half of the twentieth century, another association between violence against the Black body haunts public imagination and involves the circulation of images, including television footage, surveillance cameras, and school photos, specifically involving the child. Perhaps the most notable case involves Emmett Till.

The Christmas day photograph taken by his mother a year before his death now stands as the representative image of Emmett Till. Another image of Till served as a call to action for a generation, an "unforgettable symbol that mobilized a generation of activists" (Harold and DeLuca 271). As Harold and DeLuca suggest, a rhetorical intervention was the use of the violated Black body when a mother made a painful choice:

> The "shock waves" produced by the corpse of Emmett Till in the mid-1950s continue to reverberate powerfully in the memory of those exposed to it. We suggest that they do so, in large part, because of the forcefulness of the image of the human body in peril. The dissemination and reception of this image—of the severely mutilated face of a child—illustrates the rhetorical and political force of images in general and of the body specifically. (266)

Barbara Bennett Woodhouse suggests that the "impact on children was profound, as we know from the many movement memoirs that identify Emmett Till's murder as a crucial moment in their education about racism and the personal peril to children like themselves of racial violence" (134).

The understanding of the Till image's reception and legacy remains complicated, however, as illuminated by the recent controversy about the Dana Schutz's *Open Casket* painting as well as the associations invoked by Ti-Rock Moore's piece *Black Death Spectacle* in which the white artist incorporated a replica of teenager Michael Brown's dead body. Christina Sharpe counters the dominant narrative about the significance of the Till image to the civil rights movement as a vehicle for reaching white audiences and returns to the initial impact of the Black audience of *Jet* magazine: "At the heart of the current controversy . . . is not so much cultural appropriation or free speech, but rather intimacy and our different relationships to violence. . . . Representation in art is an arena of conflict and confrontation for Black people. . . . Dana Schutz walked into that, and what we're seeing are vigorous responses" (qtd. in Mitter). As for the protesters, she adds, they are 'keeping watch with the dead, practicing a kind of care.'" The issues are not only about who produces the images but how the images presented and to which audiences. Sharpe continues:

> I'm very interested in how the painting functions versus how the actual photographs of Emmett Till function. Mamie Till Mobley makes the decision, against much advice, to have those photographs of her son published. It was not mainstream media—or white media—that published those images. It was Jet magazine. And those images had nothing to do with white consciousness. They were for Black people, because Jet was a Black publication. They weren't meant to create empathy or shame or awareness from white viewers. They were meant to speak to and to move a Black audience. (qtd. in Mitter)

Sharpe's comment on the initial intention of the Till photos posits that the image's original dissemination was meant to mobilize Black audiences. The connection between the traumatic experience and the Black audience is then witnessed by the world at large, and that connection is essential to preserve. The activists in the Shutz protest recreate the initial encounter between Till and the Black audience, substituting this connection as the art in place of the painting. In that performance, outside audiences were forced to confront their distance or remove from the original image, complicating the relationship between image and audience in a racialized public space.

Looking at these issues of depiction and reception of Blackness in a visual realm, particularly violation of the Black child or youth in a post–civil rights context, *The Gimmick* straddles two time periods: its setting in the late sixties and seventies and its mid-nineties audiences. However, something changes between this time and the period in which *The Gimmick* is staged during the late 1990s. The Black child's violated body does not have the same rhetorical position in the political climate of late-twentieth-century America. Patricia Hill Collins offers cautionary words for the visibility that devolves from words and liberating connections to a creative community. Stemming from the global audience dissemination of hip hop and commodification (new Gimmick) of urban suffering and survival, "What are the effects on Black American youth of being simultaneously so ignored and so visible?," asks Collins. The forms of hypervisibility that attempt to contain loss but also suggest that the culture has become inured to these images. The period between included, for example, the circulation of images in the Atlanta Child Murders case when families gather around nightly newscasts and see the uncensored images of Black children's lifeless bodies pulled from the river, and the controversy remains in today's social media context when videos circulate depicting violated Black bodies, including Black children such as Tamir Rice.

To redirect his fixed view on traumatic representations, Alexis offers her own vulnerability and allows him to paint her nude. The conversations between Alexis and Jimmy here seem to suggest this tension between choosing to "mirror" the internal pain of "what's taking place" and becoming an "ally" to "the forces of liberation" as Charles White describes. Alexis, a young Black writer, appears to discourage the depiction of negative emotions from a young male visual artist. Jimmy always had both a joyful innocence and an emptiness. Alexis wants Jimmy to see beyond his pain and into a future that includes an enriching environment. He paints the body she longs to see reflected to her. He changes his subject matter in part to please Alexis, and it seems initially to uplift him and connect him to possibility. With Alexis, Jimmy painted her fullness in celebration; she was a Picasso woman. "The world was endless," she tells us: "Endless strokes of paint. / Endless words on paper. / How endless the world was" (91). Theirs was a bond of image and word. As a painter, he created the visual while she told the story behind it or promised to tell it. In their intimacy, there was no disconnect between the visual realm and the narrative that addressed its truth as well. The "endless" quality that they felt through their collaboration stands in clear contrast to the limited horizon lived out by their parents and represented by the trap of the "gimmick" or addiction.

Painting her body as precious in gold, Jimmy tells her: "You my muse / you my muse, Alexis girl' / glowing / glowing / he gives me my portrait / a swirl of colors / not just Orange Red Black and Blue / my portrait was gold / I saw gold / I was gold / 'now everybody can see it, Alexis / How beautiful you are'" (91). His art connects to a repeated imagery related to "gold" with gold paint, seeming to idealize Alexis, suggesting that he moves between extremes, trapped in a binary between sacred and profane or desecrated, the rigid dichotomies of a posttraumatic sensibility and in contrast to Alexis, who privileges the nuance in her experience and its contradictory elements. Their connection is a healing force but one that does not have sustainability when faced with the outside world when it co-opts the image.

In this way too Jimmy's artistic renderings, including Alexis's portrait, lose something essential when he delivers to white audiences in a way that does not incorporate all the historical complexities of the Black female nude in public space reinforces/reproduces a kind of violence or denial of the original relationship. The "portrait was gold" because it was created in a space of Black intimacy that countered the deadening force of the "gimmick" which stands in many ways for the structural racism causing the urban blight and despair. Also, Jimmy's painting of Alexis to redirect his expression of pain seems also to be the source of his undoing when he relies too heavily on Alexis for his well-being.

Their connection countered the invisibility and irrelevance they felt in the face of the Gimmick to which their parents had succumbed. As young Black artists, they had to create a new world from their imaginations and their love for each other. The scenes between them center on an innocence, reclaiming an innocence or "blank canvas" on which to generate a new world. *The Gimmick's* Jimmy and Alexis resemble this artistic comradeship in their early days together, but we see the overwhelming sense of isolation threaten to destroy Alexis too initially when she loses her contact with Jimmy. She posed for the painting and exposed herself, made herself vulnerable, because it was a gesture of connection to each other and gave her a sense of being witnessed, of having someone see her body in its beauty and realness without being immersed in ideological trappings. Deborah E. McDowell writes that "if any group has had the need historically of resisting and revising, subverting and controlling their bodies and their body images, Black women have, for our bodies have never been our bodies; our 'selves' have never been ourselves." Art historian Lisa Collins turns to Judith Wilson's work in *Black Popular Culture*—"Getting Down to Get Over: Romare Beardon's Use of Pornography and the Problem of the Black Female Nude in Afro-American Art" and points out Wilson's observation regarding the lack of Black female nudes in nineteenth-century art with Sara Baartman's and Josephine Baker's hypersexualized and exoticized bodies appearing most frequently. The other rare occasion occurs when, Collins explains:

abolitionists in the United States adopted an image of a partially clad female supplicant framed by the words "Am I Not a Woman and a Sister?" Strategically targeted at women, this image appeared in the women's section of newspapers, as well as on popular art forms such as tokens, dishware, and textiles sold by antislavery women at fundraising events. Shown on her knees, bare breasted, and in chains, this icon explicitly linked nudity with vulnerability and slavery with sexual violence in order to outrage women and press them to agitate for abolition. (102)

In more contemporary manifestations, Elaine B. Richardson remarks, "There is hardly a media outlet to which a Black woman can turn and not see a negative image of herself.... Music videos, television talk shows, news shows, newspapers, and tabloids show us as one-sided and oft times disfigured representations of African American females: pulsating genitals, hood rats, 'successful' professional sisters, alienated in corporate America or the academy, low-income mothers, falling stars" (74).

When she loses her painting, Alexis experiences a deep loss of connection to the artistic representation of her experience. Her reaction to the selling of her image is also linked to her reception at the art gallery. She felt that she was not welcome. The contrast between the real Black young woman feeling like a spectacle, unwelcomed, and judged, and the desirability of her body on a canvas is significant. The sale of the painting created a breach between image and word, a vulnerability that had been exploited or that conjured up earlier moments in history. Alexis has already faced internalized hatred and felt alienated from her body, and she feels unrecognized by her mother, Lenny, who exists in a limbo, trapped by the expectation that she becomes relevant only through a male relationship: "Sometimes when I talked to her she didn't hear me / she's looking out the window / smoking and waiting" (79). Lenny interrupts her dreaming and longing for her past self, the one who appealed to men, only to subject

Alexis's body to terrible scrutiny. She weighs her and measures her worth according to her physical appeal. She's flesh to be assessed based on her desirability: "I'm eight or nine or nine or eleven / I'm on the scale / my flesh measured by numbers / 'disgusting,' she says / her words were worse than the sting her belt / her words / my mother Lenny's words left invisible welts / scars / her words / when I close my eyes / made me think of Orange Red Black Blue / I wanted soft words / kind words / words that when I close my eyes made me think of caresses and kisses" (80). Feeling objectified and unworthy, Alexis explains within her diary: "God made me big and fatter than other kids and it makes me feel bad when people call me fatty and I cry sometimes I wonder where people go when they die . . . sometimes I want to disappear" (80). She experiences a desire to be heard, yet she also wants to disappear because her body's current difference from societal expectations causes her shame.

Even before her portrait's sale, they go to the gallery. The nude portraits of Alexis are on the wall, and Jimmy feels a sense of validation in the exposure: "He swirls / whirls / dances / jumps / 'I'm an artist, Alexis / I'm fifteen years old and I'm a real artist'" (93). They also want to look the part as "real artists." Alexis's encounter with Genevieve invokes her insecurities about her body, and "Genevieve knows the world likes thin skinny girls / skinny / thin / white Modigliani girls / the world does not like big / Black / girls at all / not at all" (95). Alexis feels confident in her "Annie Hall" outfit as she makes her way downtown to Jimmy's show: "I'm walking the Harlem streets feeling strong and cool. . . . I get there strong and cool" (95); however, the portrait of Genevieve she encounters in the gallery reawakens her self-doubt and the concern that Genevieve will replace her as Jimmy's Paris companion. Alexis observes the wealth and whiteness of the gallery attendees with "tight smiles" and TV hair (96). "Jimmy, are you really from Harlem?" Alexis overhears one person ask, as if it seemed unlikely or impossible to connect Harlem with the giftedness demonstrated in his work, and this assessment furthers the sense of estrangement experienced by Alexis in the gallery. Mirroring Genevieve, Jimmy takes on the affect and mannerisms guided to denote sophistication. Alexis feels like an outsider watching her closest relationship behave like a stranger: "I'm pushed out" (97). Jimmy surrenders to the crowd's demands while Alexis leaves the gallery, dejected: "I want to go back to Harlem / I want to go back to my house / decrepit / violent / I don't belong down here" (97). When she arrives home, she feels estranged from that place as well. She had believed that Jimmy and she had found a home within their relationship, but now she remains outside of his world and lost.

Jimmy's paintings depict both his suffering and his hope and journey into meaning in the form of Alexis's nude. Once the painting leaves the sanctity of their relationship, the circulation of these representations produces anxiety and becomes fraught within a cultural context that has not valued the Black body in the same way. Is it any wonder that the idea of her image circulating beyond her control caused Alexis to spiral into chaos? *The Gimmick* is conjuring something that resonates, some residue of experience that accompanies the connection between the circulating image of the explicit body of the Black child and a terrible anxiety. The severance of Alexis's relationship to Jimmy is the disconnection between the circulating image and its original narrative when the image and language disconnect.

To save herself and contain this overwhelming anxiety, Alexis returns to the archive, represented in her relationship with Ms. Innis, the Harlem librarian. This return suggests that she will not only continue to pursue her dreams but will also do so connected to both past and future in a literary community that tells the story behind these freely circulating images. In the first moments of the play as she announces Jimmy's death, Ms. Innis, the librarian, and the only person other than Jimmy to see Alexis for her gifts, describes the paradoxical nature of the surroundings: "I'm looking at Mt. Morris Park again as I write this / there is darkness but behind it there is beauty / there is light" (73). These lines are repeated at the play's end, along with a reversal: "Mt. Morris Park / bright and sunny today but there is always darkness underneath" (107). This time, however, Ms. Innis's words are interwoven with Alexis's poetry, demonstrating Alexis's incorporation of the pain involved in her surroundings with her artistic voice. She has turned the ghetto into song. Before Alexis can reclaim her words, she must move through the crisis caused by the break in her relationship with Jimmy, the breach between his images and her stories.

Earlier, Alexis establishes a relationship with Ms. Innis, showing her poems that she has started writing. Although she struggles initially to accept Ms. Innis's kindness and sincere interest in her development as a young writer, her craving for real connection wins. Alexis finds Evelyn Tooley Hunt's "My Mother Taught Me Purple," a poem that speaks to the necessity of creative expression and links an ancestral relationship to the value: "My mother reached for beauty / And for its lack she died" (87) Alexis believes that to live authentically in this work, she must cultivate her ability to be a "word magician" (87), and the library provides a sanctuary for Alexis to engage in a creative life. Tea, sandwiches, and recognition of her potential as a writer allow Alexis to thrive as she navigates the Gimmicks and returns to her mother's apartment.

Jimmy's struggle to channel the creative energy as a shield against the Gimmicks becomes clear; even after Jimmy finds a creative home at Mr. Kaufman's studio, in the midst of this newfound joy, he continues to feel the nag of self-doubt: "Maybe I can't, Alexis / maybe I don't deserve to do good" (89). Alexis serves as his touchstone, reminding Jimmy in his moments of doubt that he remains worthy and has authentic artistic talent. Even with Alexis's reassurance, Jimmy "lights a joint" (89). When Alexis responds with "Naw Naw, Jimmy, you don't need it" (89), it becomes clear that she recognizes the relationship between a lingering pain and self-medication. In the early '70s downtown New York art scene, Jimmy would encounter many opportunities for recreational drug use, but the link between his expression of self-doubt and the substance use signals that Jimmy remains unable to shake the Gimmick. As Alexis feels Jimmy slipping away, she identifies her angry, destructive urges as "my Gimmick is strong" (97). The Gimmick emerges in a confrontation with a random white girl, whose attempt at a friendly smile appears as taunting to Alexis. Alexis struggles with the disconnect between her angry display and attempt to threaten the girl by blocking her from passing and her inner despair that feels helpless: "Inside I say, 'my God what am I doing / she seems nice'" (98). This exchange reveals an aspect of the "Gimmick" that involves an estrangement from self and an authentic connection to the source of one's pain. The Gimmick provokes violence at victims by association and flattens nuance and distinction. It forces a release as a misfire or misdirection, so no comfort can follow, but the person caught up becomes compromised. The Gimmick is becoming inhabited by a negative force that distorts agency.

After an ugly argument with Jimmy, in which she admits that the situation with Genevieve has stirred up a rage in her, she finds herself lost: "I wish I were invisible" (99). Jimmy fails to recognize that Alexis feels abandoned by him. He confirms that he has chosen Genevieve because she has influence and can advance his art career. The loss fills Alexis with hate when she can feel at all. She even loses her relationship with words: "Words mean nothing / books just reflect / don't change / it's not real / I can't take words in / don't care to take words in / in my journal I write disappear / disappear" (99). For Alexis, art and creativity remain tied to her friendship with Jimmy. The two sources of self-worth need each other to exist, and then she needs them together to feel present as well.

Ms. Innis recognizes that Alexis has lost herself to grief, and she encounters a drunk Lenny when she seeks to support Alexis at her home. In this moment, Alexis understands the contrast between her birth mother and the librarian who connects her to a cultural archive and sense of her own burgeoning relationship to the written word. While Lenny is "Gimmicking the proper lady," Alexis views Miss Innis as more authentic: "Ms. Innis was a true lady / she, Lenny, knew it / tried to emulate it / she, Lenny, couldn't touch it" (100). As part of her mentoring, Miss Innis offers Alexis a way to shape reality and breathe possibility into a moment of despair: "I know how deeply you feel this hurt / Alexis, you need to feel it / then use it / put it into words / like James Baldwin" (100). Miss Innis renders a portrait of Alexis as a young artist, rather than an object for the Gimmicks to use: "You are an artist, Alexis," she asserts, quoting Tolstoy: "Art is not a handicraft. It is a transmission of feeling experienced by the artist" (100). The advice Ms. Innis offers Alexis stands in contrast to Alexis's earlier attempts to steer Jimmy away from his expression of more negative, complex emotions. In this way, Jimmy's downfall may seem related to his inability to draw on the reservoir of feeling, to transmit his pain, transformed through art. Jimmy finds himself within another Gimmick, one inadvertently supported by Alexis. The Gimmick here, as with other Gimmicks, entails the corruption or distortion of emotion while the creation of art requires self-regulation and awareness.

Jimmy's downward spiral is represented as a painter losing his color: "Jimmy comes to the house one day . . . colorless / no color around him / not shining / no glow" (101). He returns to apologize, it seems at first; however, as the loss of color indicates, he needs something to replenish him, and he asks for the painting to be returned, so that he can sell it. He comes back asking for forgiveness, but then he follows with a request for the portrait he gave her, and she acquiesces as she feels a sense of connection still to their earlier synergy: "I go / I get it / my portrait / Jimmy gave me a piece of myself / now he's taking it away / myself / he's taking it away" (102). When Alexis sees Jimmy entering Tootsie's place, she despairs. He has entered the "house of Gimmicks" and

Resiliency and the Crisis of the Black Child's Image in *The Gimmick* 75

the "anything for money Gimmick." She compares Jimmy to the addicted people and does not believe he belongs there. They have already lost everything to their addiction, "but Jimmy's got everything to lose" (102). However, the history of the "Got nothin' to lose people" is unknown to Alexis. From her perspective, Jimmy stands apart as exceptional. She chooses to join him, rather than risk losing him entirely, and does not reflect on her choice as one that has occurred many times before. Jimmy found early success, but he had never addressed the underlying self-doubt about his worthiness.

When she enters Tootsie's place, she encounters a world of lost souls, and Jimmy aligns himself with them: "And I can't believe he's defending a Darkman / Gangster man over me" (103). Alexis faces a crisis in which she almost loses all the promise and hope that her connection to creativity has given her. For Alexis, her own survival as an artist seems intertwined with Jimmy's: "We were gonna put the Gimmicks behind us / Gonna throw everything away." Against the earlier advice from Miss Innis, Alexis offers to lose herself alongside Jimmy: "You wanna test me, see how far I'll go? / For you . . . I'd give up my love for language / words / I'd give up words / I'd kill the colors in me / my words / emotions / thoughts / they'd no longer be words / mumbles 'n' grunts / mumbles 'n' grunts" (103). Alexis faces an impossible choice between her first sense of love and her connection to the creative drive at the core of her being. Tragedy imbues this moment as it illuminates the internal struggle faced when a loved one, particularly one that has an integral role in the dream of escape and realizing a potential life devoted to artistic freedom. The moment bears witness to the relationship between trauma and addiction as the flip side to creative expression to navigate complex, often trauma-induced emotions. As they descend into mutual destruction, Jimmy awakens from his dope coma to see his father raping Alexis, and instead of trying to save her, he grabs the bag of dope Clarence throws his way to quiet him. This betrayal marks a devastating end to their relationship. Jimmy has already died because of the dope. His apologies mean nothing, and Alexis sees herself as nothing in her beloved friend's eyes. Lenny later tries to support her daughter by bringing her to church, but Alexis does not find any healing there, referring to it as a "new House of Gimmicks . . . God he's a Gimmick" (104). The Gimmick always has an element of the external and takes away agency by locating it outside of oneself. She returns home and begins to cut up the clothes she wore during the rape: "I bring them to my neck / want to slice myself / waste myself . . . I see the empty space / the space where my portrait was / where myself was / I gave him myself in the portrait / he took it / now I'm looking at the wall where it was / the space / empty" (105–6). This identification of the portrait with her value and her authentic self illuminates the nature of her crisis and the way she must return to claim herself within language and not in relation to anyone else's view of her worth.

Another writer's influence silences the voices telling her to take her own life. She refers to herself repeatedly in her despair as a "waste"; however, the book reminds her of Ms. Innis's words: "Use words / do not waste" (106). The relationship with James Baldwin saves her, sustains her. In their 1964 pamphlet, "Youth in the Ghetto: A Study of the Consequences of Powerlessness and a Blueprint for Change," Harlem Youth Opportunities Unlimited, Inc. identifies the immeasurability of the loss when youth voices lose their chance to be heard: "90 percent of the young people are not overtly delinquent. These nondelinquent youth can not be ignored. We have no data on the price they are required to pay in hopelessness and despair. We have no way of calculating the social costs inherent in the wastage of their human, creative potentials." This calculation reveals itself in *The Gimmick* through Alexis's direct encounter with the waste that has become Jimmy's existence and that threatens her own life. Alexis had initially believed that she had "invented" herself through the relationship with Jimmy and that the portrait signified his ability to see the self that included her aspirations and potential: "I reach for my pen / I reach for language / for the words in me / those words will make me beautiful strong / will make Jimmy beautiful strong / will create beauty" (106). There is the sense of loss, the grief and guilt that accompany survival. Alexis tells the story of her friendship with Jimmy and their shared dream to escape the Gimmicks through their creativity. What does "survivor's guilt" mean here? She has already given up on her mother and does not mention any other family on which to lean. Survival and art, the art of survival, and art that bears witness to survival: survival is linked to the creative imaginary.

Alexis develops the ability to create alternative spaces and exist, when necessary, in them and through them. Perhaps the most powerful example of these generative strategies involves her imaginary connection to the writer James Baldwin to guide her in his representation of Blackness and artistry as an expatriate in Paris. She thinks back to their childhood hopes and owns its beauty, even to sustain her without Jimmy's presence: "With knees clasped to our chins we huddled on the stoop together / swearing / when we grow up we could do it / you and me / we can do it us / you / me / together / gonna put this ghetto thing down / gonna turn our back on this ghetto thing" (88).

Alexis writes about liberation and surpassing boundaries, but the "voices" perhaps represent the internal obstructions to freedom, whether they exist within herself or within her immediate community or family as internalized limitations on her possibility: "If I could unlock all the doors / break all the locks / break down doors and locks / I'd come out / but I hear voices / and the voices / the voices are hard / I retreat again" (88). In her efforts to comfort Alexis after Jimmy's death, Ms. Innis tells her, "Paris, they say, is beautiful this time of year" (107). Her poetry claims the beauty of her portrait and the space it leaves behind, in Harlem's streets and in telling its story with all of the sights and sounds revealing "the souls of young boys and girls are trapped underneath the hoods of stolen cars" (109). For Alexis, "love is something cranked up real loud on the dilapidated stereo for everybody in the streets to hear" (110). Through the experience Alexis has gained an emotional literacy that puts the Gimmicks' ability to capture her spirit at risk. In this discovery toward a kind of self-regulation, she mirrors Audre Lorde's well-known observations on poetry's essential value: "We can train ourselves to respect our feelings, and to discipline (transpose) them into a language that matches those feelings so they can be shared. And where that language does not yet exist, it is our poetry which helps to fashion it" (37). She has taken the risk of remaining connected through literature against the soul-deadening lure of the Gimmicks.

In the next chapter, Precious extends this embrace of language and benefits from the wave of Black women writers that Alexis joins in the 1970s–80s who express their desire to look specifically at intimate spaces in their lives while also returning to literary foremothers unmarked graves.

CHAPTER 3

POSTTRAUMATIC LITERACIES AND THE MATERIAL BODY IN SAPPHIRE'S *PUSH*

I think about being a poet or rapper or an artist even.
—Precious Jones, *Push*

In 2016, the National Women's Law Center released the Let Her Learn campaign with an accompanying "Toolkit to Stop School Push Out for Girls of Color." Included in the Toolkit is the statistic that "Black girls are 5.5 times more likely to be suspended from school as white girls" and "Black girls are more likely than any other race or gender to be suspended more than once." According to the document, "National stats from the 2013–14 school year show that: These uneven rates of discipline are not because of more frequent or serious misbehavior." This campaign in part responded to incidents such as the Spring Valley High School assault, which received national attention when a recording circulated widely online. On October 26, 2015, a sixteen-year-old girl was placed in a chokehold and flipped over in her desk and arrested by a school resource officer for refusing to leave the classroom for chewing gum and having a cell phone on her desk. In addition, one of her classmates, Niya Kenny, was also arrested for videotaping the incident.

When Niya Kenny stood up and risked her personal safety to object to the violence and to record the incident, she served as the only true witness, documenting the abuse and disseminating the truth beyond the classroom walls. If left to the school officials, the story would not have been released to the public, and the police officer would not have faced accountability for the excessive force. "Niya's case alone is simply a powerful example about how leadership skills and courage and the ability to reason right from wrong . . . get turned into a justification for bringing them into the juvenile justice system," Kimberle Crenshaw responds. "[Black] girls in particular tend to run into trouble because they're seen as defiant, they're seen as having an attitude or being in need of discipline rather than being rewarded and recognized for exercising leadership" (qtd. in Klein). Niya's bravery offered an "I see YOU" that recognized the humanity of her classmate, another Black girl, who was thrown around like she had no value. The Spring Valley assault case became the story of two girls and the way in which Niya disrupted the violation with her outrage and her recording. Since the young woman at the desk was under eighteen, her name was not reported, and her face is not apparent in the video. Because of this, she becomes hypervisible in her trauma and invisible in her individual identity. As the officer attempts to wrench her body forcefully from the desk, the relationship between the body and the desk raises questions about misrecognition of Black youth in classroom spaces that have both historical and contemporary resonance.

In the culture wars of the post–civil rights era, the classroom remains a space in which the Black child is marked as "at risk." Historically, education has been the site of struggle for equal access and opportunity. The hostility facing the Black child entering the segregated classroom remains in our collective memory through visual representations such as Ruby Bridges in Norman Rockwell's painting "The Problem We All Live With," which depicts her small body sympathetically against the backdrop of a racial slur. In her lived experience, Ruby met with white mothers carrying miniature coffins with Black children within them, visual symbols of their desire to desecrate her potential. Other historical images of Black children threatened while crossing the threshold to desegregate classrooms include the Little Rock Nine, and later with the Boston bussing crisis, with a shattered bus window now on display at the Smithsonian's National Museum of American History.

In the half-century following the Brown decision, activists and educators have noted the problems remaining both through efforts to integrate and place Black children in primarily white environments as well as the continuing de facto segregation arising from redlining and "white flight." As cases such as *Sheff v. O'Neill* in Hartford, Connecticut, revealed, schools remain segregated due to "white flight," and often problems were raised about environments that were neglectful/overwhelmed with scarcity of resources or the remedy to the "achievement gap" included school as a militarized zone. The "School to Prison Pipeline" has become a phrase raised in public discourse in the aftermath and exposes the cost of these rigid, policed "educational" zones. Controversial methods intended to motivate scholars often result in militaristic environments that rely on shame and humiliation to gain results, exemplified by the controversy generated when a recording surfaced of a NYC Success Academy teacher's tearing up a young student's work in front of the entire class and berating the student (Taylor).

Published in the height of the mid-nineties culture wars, the issues raised by *Push* in relation to the Black child in the classroom remain relevant today, when schools become a "law and order" zone in which the emphasis is placed on obedience and managing bodies rather than liberating minds. The public discourse around race and education identifies that classroom as another site in which Black children find themselves marked as "at risk," and like the Spring Valley incident, *Push* reveals the paradox of hypervisibility-invisibility that shapes the young women of color's experience with educational and social service institutions.

Desks in classrooms fix students within the space in a particular arrangement, an order that contains their bodies. When the young woman in the Spring Valley assault case refused to move from her desk, she faced violent extrication. The desk anchored her within the classroom, and she claimed her place and refused to be moved. Any control or autonomy for Black girls is negated through force or imposition as this case demonstrates. In a narrative that reveals a considerable lack of choice in young Precious's life, the classroom offers a space of intervention for her full humanity to emerge and become visible with the support of other girls of color enrolled in Each One Teach One, who all gain insight into their place within systems of oppression. For Precious in particular, this transformation involves her recognition of herself as a poet sourcing identity from her deep love for language.

With this cultural context in mind, this chapter begins in the classroom. In the previous chapter, we witness the inner turmoil caused when Alexis's portrait circulates beyond the intimacy of a relationship based on shared artistic aspirations. In *Push*, Precious Jones suffers from invisibility, even as external forces seize control over her body. The research suggests that the classroom can become the site of trauma for girls of color. Precious does not experience any direct violence in the classroom, but the school leaders and teachers do not recognize her full humanity and instead view her as a problem and project value judgments without knowing her full story. The traditional school is limited in its capacity to address the full scope of Precious's needs.

As a traumatized child, Precious enters public space through educational systems and classroom spaces, and through this entry, her story becomes one for witnessing, with the classroom providing one of the first, if not the primary, community for the youth. Precious witnesses herself reborn as a poet who must first learn to navigate the complexities of her compromised relationship to language, literacy, and her own body. From its opening, *Push* connects traumatic history, bodily response, and educational deficits:

I was left back when I was twelve because I had a baby by my fahver. That was in 1983. I was out of school for a year. This gonna be my second baby. My daughter got Down Sinder. She's retarded. I got left back in second grade too, when I was seven, 'cause I couldn't read (and still peed on myself). I should be in the eleventh grade, getting reading to go into twelf' grade so I can gone 'n graduate. But I'm not. I'm in the ninfe grade. (3)

Precious tells the reader that she could not read and follows parenthetically with a disclosure that she "still peed" on herself. These two problems may have existed at the same time without influencing each other, and her lack of control over her own body processes within the classroom caused problems for her, particularly in relation to her ability to master language. Her abuse history has kept her from progressing in school, clearly, and in this introduction to her painful experience in school

Precious's history in the classroom involves a "disappearing act" in which she removes herself repeatedly through dissociation from her body. Her desk becomes an anchor to weigh her down in space while her mind leaves. She becomes inanimate, merging with the desk as an object in the classroom that has no ability to engage dynamically. School is a place of public rejection, where her classmates and teachers confirm her "not-belonging" state: "I always did like school, jus' seem school never did like me. Kinnergarden and first grade I don't talk, they laff at that.... Secon' grade they laffes at HOW I talk. So I stop talking" (36). She is mocked by the students and believes that the teacher hates her. She remains in her seat and wets herself because she does not want to get up and face the ridicule:

> Secon' grade is when I just start to sit there. All day. Other kids run all around. Me, Clareece P. Jones, come in at 8:55, sit down, don't move till the bell ring to go home. I wet myself. Don't know why I don't get up, but I just don't. I jus' sit there and pee. Teacher ack all

care at first, then scream, then get Principal. Principal call Mam and who else I don't remember. Finally Principal say, Let it be. Be glad thas all the trouble she give you. Focus on the ones who *can* learn, Principal say to teacher. What does that mean? Is he one of the ones who can't? (37)

Precious closes down and restricts her movement. In posttraumatic response, there is a narrowing down of one's perspective and movement, a freezing of affect and motion in automatic self-protection. Precious fixes herself to her desk in a kind of catatonic state. Her responses are misread by the teacher and principal, and they treat her like a piece of furniture instead of a living child in desperate need of an intervention to bring her back to her body. This auto-response involves no conscious decision-making process at this point. The lack of care about her experience provides insight into how she was able to get through middle school without knowing how to read. Even as her body sent direct signals of her distress to the school authorities, she received a label as "hopeless" and beyond the reach of education.

When she does not move from her desk, she remains "safe" but also does not participate in shaping the narrative around her own experience, except through her passivity, which is mislabeled as deadness/inertia. Although the dissociation may have provided a way to survive her sexual abuse from her parents, this response proves maladaptive in her school environment.

Bruce Perry explains:

> If, during development, the threat response apparatus is persistently stimulated, a commensurate stress response apparatus develops in the central nervous system in response to the constant threat. These stress-response neural systems (and all the functions they mediate) are overactive and hypersensitive. It is highly adaptive for a child growing up in a violent, chaotic environment to be hypersensitive to external stimuli, hypervigilant, and in a persistent stress-response

state. These adaptive changes in the brain make a child better suited to sense, perceive, and act on threat in such an environment, but these "survival tactics" ill serve the child when the environment changes (as at school or in peer relationships). (24)

Katie Statman-Weil refers to her experience with a young girl named Christina when addressing the effect of traumatic histories on the classroom dynamic:

> Children who have experienced early trauma may have a hard time listening and concentrating in class because they dissociate or freeze when their stress responses are triggered by sounds, smells, or behaviors that remind them of the trauma. Christina tends to dissociate if someone touches her when she does not expect it, even when it is meant as a friendly touch, such as a pat on the back. The teacher does not recognize this behavior as dissociation and instead views Christina as a daydreamer. She often goes unnoticed in the classroom because when her stress response is triggered, rather than make a loud commotion, Christina silently withdraws into herself. Christina's so-called daydreaming—her withdrawal behavior—leaves her as vulnerable to falling behind academically. (77)

Trauma scholars have known for a while that trauma causes disturbances in the brain's language centers but have only recently started understanding how this all plays out in children. Sapphire's novel fictionalizes an experience about which trauma research, particularly when intersected with education scholarship, remains in an active state of discovery. That is, how dissociation and the feelings of being estranged from one's bodily present interfere with learning and how reintegration occurs in relation to placing oneself within a community, a larger narrative, and exceeding the rigidity of post-traumatic response.

    Chalkboard, tests, desks, books—these material objects of learning interact with the body. Precious needs to use them to fasten her to the present although they initially threaten her, causing her to dissociate. What does it mean to dissociate when faced with the actual material objects and activities of learning? Like Christina, Precious demonstrates the struggles of the abused child to negotiate the school system and to control the interference of her abuse on her ability to learn in the present:

> And the daytimes don't make no sense. Don't make sense talking, bouncing balls, filling in between dotted lines. Shape? Color? Who cares whether purple shit a square or circle, whether it purple or blue? What difference it make whether gingerbread house on top or bottom of the page. I disappear from the day, I jus' put it all down—book, doll, jump rope, my head, myself. I don't think I look up again until EMS find me on the floor. (18)

School devotes itself to shapes, colors, and organizing the world in language-symbols, but her world defies organizational schemas. Dissociation does not align with the top/bottom, circle/square logic.

For Precious, this estrangement within the classroom results in feeling hypervisible in her shame and as a "problem" while sensing erasure in relation to the testing measurements imposed on her: "The tesses paint a picture of me wif no brain. The tesses paint a picture of me an' my muver—my whole family, we more than dumb, we invisible" (30). Precious is a member of what Patricia Hill Collins calls the "hip hop generation." When describing Precious's generation, Collins suggests that "this is a generation whose actual members remain written off, marginalized, and largely invisible in everyday life. Isolated and ghettoized within American society" (3). *Push* deals with these issues related to the Black child and violence both within a family structure that has been shaped by internalized and institutional racism (and sexism). We witness others reacting to Precious's body as abject, as material for their own use or projection. We see, for instance, the response of the guidance counselor to Precious is initially disgust and blame-throwing.

Deborah E. McDowell's assertion that "the body became the site of black women's subjection and, simultaneously, the route to their agency and liberation" (299) appears significant and relevant when considering an adolescent girl such as Precious as well. This subjection is seen for Precious in her home, at school, in the street, everywhere she goes, except her own mind. The intense, constant assaults on Precious's body stand in for a generation or for larger social concerns. A few incredible moments clearly depict the degradation of the Black girl's body: Mary Jones kicks her daughter's head while she is in labor, and her father, Carl, smacks her during sex. She gets into a physical altercation with her mother shortly after giving birth and needs to flee with her newborn child. She finds herself at the homeless shelter, blanket stolen from her body, still bleeding from birth. Precious's description of the ghetto suggests the treatment of her own body: people use it for their own gain, exploited, abused. She cannot cross a street without a man yelling "Scarf" about her eating while other students make pig noises at her.

Throughout the narrative, Precious reiterates her sense of spiritual invisibility due to her abuse and her identity as a young poor Black woman: "I big, I talk, I eats, I cooks, I laugh, watch TV, do what my muver says. But I can see when the picture comes back I don't exist" (31). She feels her agency bubbling to the surface but remaining trapped as she navigates her way through the Harlem streets: "I wanna say I am somebody. I wanna say it on the subway, TV, movie, LOUD. I see pink faces in suits look over top of my head. I watch myself disappear in their eyes, their tesses. I talk loud but still I don't exist" (31). She names her abjectness and through her naming, enters the scene: "Don't nobody want me." Precious identifies herself as "Don't nobody need me. I know who I am. I know who they say I am—vampire sucking the system's blood. Ugly black grease to be wipe away, punish, kilt, changed, finded a job for" (31), exhibiting profound self-awareness of the role she plays in the neoliberal schema of the post–civil rights era and nineties welfare reform. Her boundaries blur within her self-awareness as well, indicating the way this pervasive abuse threatens her integrity: "Why can't I see myself, *feel* where I end and begin. I sometimes look in the pink people in suits eyes, the men from bizness, and they look way above me, put me out of their eyes" (32). When she identifies this crisis with her boundaries, she invents a site of inquiry where none existed previously. Her self-reflection urges an examination of the relationship between her struggle with invisibility and her creative drive to bring forth a representation in language that connects to her experience. She articulates the tension between feeling seen and feeling judged: "I look bitch teacher woman in the face, trying to see do she see *me* or the tess. But I don't care now what anybody see. I see something, somebody. I got baby. So what. I feel proud 'cept it's baby by my fahver and that make me not in the picture again" (33). Precious defines "in the picture" here as someone who remains acceptable by conventional standards, someone who does not have a taboo history.

Many references to visibility occur throughout the novel, with distinct purposes but with a shared resonance about the way *Push* navigates materializing subject: "I'm just so tired I jus' want to disappear" (11), "Can't he see I am a girl for flowers and thin straw legs and a place in the picture" (32) and "Sometimes I pass by store window and somebody fat dark skin, old looking, someone look like my muver look back at me" (32). The boundary issues caused by the abuse, dissociation, and the cultural stereotypes, create a crisis in her identity. She cannot even see herself.

Precious expresses a sense of complete estrangement and alienation from mainstream culture. The relationship between traumatic dissociation and imagination appears in Precious's ability to dream herself into new realities and suggests a burgeoning artistic capacity. In "'Maybe I'll Be a Poet, Rapper': Hip-Hop Feminism and Literary Aesthetics in *Push*," Brittney Cooper notes that "*Push* foregrounds and is informed by a hip-hop aesthetic. This aesthetic issues from a generational confrontation with economic lack, privation, and the realities of civil rights–era dreams deferred" (56) and "*Push* calls into existence a new generation of black women's stories, stories that consider age-old of questions of family, motherhood, friendship, sex, and love, but in the context of hip-hop culture, the AIDS epidemic, the conservative backlash of the 1980s, and the deindustrialized city confronting urban blight" (55). Before she begins reading, Precious finds resources for resilience and alternatives to her plot in the media. Precious's imagination and her strategies of survival through fantasy as she tries to place her body in a new world and more active, creative scenarios. We see her dance, think of herself as Janet Jackson, as someone who looks beautiful in certain colors. Precious imagines herself into the plot: "Everyday I tell myself something gonna happen, some shit like on TV. I'm gonna break through or somebody gonna break through to me—I'm gonna learn, catch up, be normal, change my seat to the front of the class. But again, it has not been that day" (5). She imagines a reality separate and different from her current existence and tries to find a new plot in which to insert herself and turns to media—to television, specifically—because this screen life is the only narrative-generating medium she knows. Her strategies show a survivor's pursuit of a new symbolic order by which to shape the chaos of trauma into meaning. These moments provide a glimpse into Precious's creative possibility when we see her revise her role within these media scripts. For example, she employs media-supported dissociation during abuse: "Then I change the stations, change *bodies*, I be dancing in videos! In movies! I be breaking, *fly*, jus' a dancing! Umm hmm heating up the stage at the Apollo for Doug E. Fresh or Al B. Sure! They love me!" (24). Black urban culture's rich expression during the 80s and 90s hip hop explosion provides Precious with resources to imagine herself beyond the abuse. The energy and vitality of the arts allows vicarious agency.

From the beginning, Precious reflects on the possibility of narrative and story-telling, to both escape life's limitations with the narrative flexibility and to bring the truth of experience to light. Her relationship to words and language includes critical inquiry, such as questioning the reasoning behind the term "Indian summer" (4). She self-protects by lashing out at her teacher while also revealing her self-awareness about this choice:

> I didn't want to hurt or embarrass him like that you know. But I couldn't let him, anybody, know page 122 look like page 152, 22, 3, 6, 5—all the pages look alike to me. 'N I really want to learn. Everyday I tell myself something going to happen, some shit like on TV. I'm gonna break through or somebody going to break through to me—I'm going to learn, catch up, be normal, change my seat to the front of the class. But again, it has not been that day. (5)

Precious has not surrendered to the forces that overdetermine her existence as abject or beyond hope. Precious's desires echo an earlier poem by Langston Hughes, the Harlem poet who will continue to inspire and shape her development as a writer. She too is a daughter of Harlem and "sings America" as an aspirational target.

This strategy of moving through existing plots beyond herself may offer a temporary reprieve, but Precious finds a true source to reinvent herself in the alternative school, where she finds a new language, a poetic justice to render her visible and present. After learning the definition of alternative, she understands implicitly her readiness to embrace change: "She asks me if I could get used to something else. I don't say nuffin', then I say a loud 'YES'" (33). When Precious sits in the classroom, Ms. Rain asks the students to introduce themselves. Precious shares that this experience of self-reflection within the classroom is new to her. Ms. Rain asks how she feels, to which Precious responds, "Here." In this direct declaration of presence, Precious occupies her body in the small student desk and claims an integrated self in the "here." Precious claims her seat, which entails participating in a community, specifically one of learners who have similar abuse histories. Noteworthy too is that each young woman within the room has a story marked by absence of a connection to a mother and must reinvent herself. The moment gestures toward a commitment to experiencing her presence in her own body and finds a kind of safety through to past bodies through intertextuality. *Push* has been referred to as a novel about literacy, but this literacy operates on many levels, including a literacy of the body, particularly the body recovering from trauma.

In *Push* the humanity of the girls of color in the classroom becomes apparent through their recognition of each other. They see each other and listen to each other and come to life within the collective space shaped by their drive, desires, and the willingness to be present with each other, to counter the invisibility marking their previous educational experiences. Elizabeth McNeil writes, "Though Precious is abused sexually, physically, verbally, and emotionally by her parents, impregnated twice by her father, ignored by protective institutions, illiterate, and ejected from the public school system, she puts up a magnificent fight to assert agency—for herself as an autonomous being and mother, for her child, and ultimately also for her community of sister survivor-activists" (14). Literacy here would involve a new kind, one that connects her separate floating pieces, grounds them in the present. Through poetry and its divergent thinking that connects unlike parts to create new meaning, Precious fastens herself together, naming the ways she leaves her body and her experiences with dissociation. Precious is ready for an arrangement, a set of values or practices, outside of the norm. She does not appear to desire a way into the norm at a certain point because she seems to have a clear understanding that sustaining or investing in a norm always involves boundaries that exclude.

Learning to read her body's language when dissociating is part of her journey toward literacy and poetry. Her artistic journey and development of this identity are deeply linked to literacy related to her abuse. She dissociates while walking to a new school and then identifies directly that she has lost track of time and space when she asks herself: "How I git here?" (25). Her mind returns to abuse when she walks down the street toward her new school. She begins thinking about pregnancy. She reverts to dissociation, unable to claim her body in the moment, such as in the scene when she tries to read aloud and then wishes that she could feel her father's abuse simply to secure herself to the present, to feel something in her body and not to float away in dissociation. Literacy here is as much about body literacy—learning to read and understand her bodily responses. The connection between dissociation and literacy is also made when she talks about urinating on herself as a second grader. Also, she faces this zoning out when at the blackboard in class. When Ms. Rain asks her about her experience on the first day of class, about actually interacting and sitting in the front row, Precious claims that it makes her feel "here,"—a simple and profound statement about occupying the present in her own body.

Even as Precious struggles with dissociation, she engages actively with the world that has influence on young people: the style and music of popular culture. One aspect of Precious's identity that gets overlooked in critical analysis of the novel is that she is sixteen and in the peak of her adolescent years and development. How much does this development stage impact the trajectory and her insights? Precious may appear to struggle with self-hatred; however, ample evidence exists to suggest that her character as an adolescent is strong, rebellious, and hopeful, driven and determined. She faces the world with spirit and determination: "Lady at Lane Bryant on one-two-five call these leggings YELLOW NEON. I'm wearing them and my X sweatshirt. Put some Vaseline on my face, nuffin' I can do about my hair until I get some money to put my braids back in. I look at my poster of Farrakhan on the wall. Amen. Allah! Radio clock glowing red 8:30 a.m. Time to go!" (22).

These moments work against a flat reading of her character and the way in which the trauma serves to determine her life. She imagines the possibility: "Maybe after I have the baby I lose some weight. Maybe I get my own place" (23). Adolescence is a time of challenges with emotional regulation. Precious has tremendous self-control in a variety of situations (and lashes out in others). She is, after all, a teenager. The instability or dynamic, chaotic nature of teenage emotional life may provide the opportunity to reject the harm, rather than internalize it.

From the novel's beginning, she starts her story and identifies herself as a truth-teller:

> My name is Claireece Precious Jones. I don't know why I'm telling you that. Guess 'cause I don't know how far I'm going with this story, or whether it's even a story or why I'm talkin'. . . . [Y]ou can do anything when you are talking or writing, it's not like living when you can only do one thing. Some people tell a story 'n it don't make no sense or be true. But I'm going to try to make sense and tell the truth, else what's the fucking use? Ain' enough lies and shit out there already?" (3–4)

When addressing clinical applications of survivor stories including *Push*, Chaya Bhuvaneswar and Audrey Shafer look at the role of burgeoning literacy: "The pre-literate person's knowledge is to be tapped, honored, and used by both educator and learner as a bridge to literacy rather than replaced with the literate legitimate knowledge" (118). Her journey is one of coming into the language to tell her story and to shape a life informed by her new relationship to poetic freedom and form: "Precious begins a new identity after her first halting attempts at poetry writing, when encouraged by Ms. Rain, she begins signing her name Precious P Jones." They state that, according to an interview with Sapphire, the P stands for "Poet" (124).

Precious crafts her own form of "critical pedagogy," a field of scholarship that emphasizes critical consciousness and counters neoliberalism's focus on individual accountability for academic success. According to critical pedagogy theorist Henry A. Giroux, "Rather than forced to participate in a pedagogy designed to up test scores and undermine forms of critical thinking, students must be involved pedagogically in critically discussing, administrating and shaping the material relations of power and ideological forces that form their everyday lives." Rather than "school choice," the "alternative school" setting of "Each One Teach One" allows Precious to find the freedom to read and create poetic texts that counter abjectness and invisibility.

Push sets up a tension between the external forces against which Precious must struggle incessantly and the development of her critical consciousness. Each crisis tests her capacity to push against the urge to become overwhelmed and to accept herself as unable to gain perspective of the way her experience operates within a larger system designed for casualties. From the beginning, Precious voices her outrage at injustice directed at herself: "I got suspended from school 'cause I'm pregnant / which I don't think is fair. I ain' did nothin'!" (3). She does not internalize a sense of shame or blame for the actions of others and expresses her righteous anger very clearly and directly. Precious must witness other people react to the news that she gave birth to her father's child at twelve. While seeking help at Harlem Hospital after her mother's attempt to beat her, Precious encounters a nurse whom she had met after her first delivery. The woman attempts to scold Precious, who responds: "Mistake? I don't think so." She names the rape and rapist as "the mistake" and claims clearly: "I think I might be the solution" (75). She makes no effort to hide her story. Instead, she answers the questions for the newborn's birth certificate plainly and clearly: "'Was you ever, I mean did you ever get to be a chile?' Thas a stupid question, did I ever get to be a chile? I *am* a chile" (13). Precious's response of claiming her status as a child reflects an implicit understanding of what Georgetown Law School's Center on Poverty and Inequality refers to as "adultification bias." In their report "Girlhood Interrupted: The Erasure of Black Girls' Childhood," the center identifies the related consequences of viewing Black girls as older, denying the innocence accompanying childhood: "In light of proven disparities in school discipline, we suggest that the perception of Black girls as less innocent may contribute to harsher punishment by educators and school resource officers. Furthermore, the view that Black girls need less nurturing, protection, and support and are more independent may translate into fewer leadership and mentorship opportunities in schools." She claims her childhood against a dominant presumption that she has been damaged to the point that her age has changed. She has been abused, and she remains a child. Does her abuse disclosure make her more vulnerable to assumptions about her developmental needs and status? In her challenge to the kind but frustrating Nurse Butter, Precious contests the view that childhood is a state of purity and innocence to be preserved or that her developmental stage can be corrupted completely.

As Precious transforms into a student and a poet, she becomes more visible to herself and others, and her relationship with her mother, one of the primary adults to fail to recognize her as a child and an individual, changes. The transition from traditional school to the alternative program marks the beginning of her transformation into literacy and poetry and serves as a catalyst for the disruption with her mother. As a character, Mary Jones remains stagnant, trapped in her limitations. Sapphire's depiction of Mary Jones, Precious's violent mother who exploits her daughter in a welfare fraud scheme is controversial. Sapphire defends her character as artistic license, indicating that she should not suffer limitations as a writer due to pressure to provide positive images of Black women: "Would Crime and Punishment have been written if Dostoevsky had felt he had to confine himself to 'positive images' of Russian youth? Would we have Kafka's Metamorphosis if he had felt he could only present 'positive images' of the Jewish family? To say that an artist's job is to produce 'positive images' is to assign them the role of propagandist" (qtd in McNeil et al., 353). Michelle Wallace supports Sapphire's artistic provocations in *Invisibility Blues* when she asserts, "Before one can interrogate the negativity of images in black feminist cultural production, one must ask the question: what makes a critical portrayal of a black person a 'negative image' if films like *Blue Velvet* and *Taxi Driver* don't count as 'negative images' of white men but rather as effective cultural expression" (4). It required a certain fearlessness to create the Mary character, and it involved creative risk in that Sapphire alienated many liberal perspectives concerned about the portrayal of Mary Jones and that it would perpetuate stereotypes in the era following Reagan's "welfare queen." As an artist, Sapphire is involved with presenting the whole spectrum of humanity and did not feel obligated to make Mary a sympathetic character. In essence, *Push* places itself intertextually in relation to *The Color Purple* and the concern that Black men were represented falsely or in a damaging way in the discussion between Ms. Rain and Precious, who aligns herself with artistic freedom.

Push leaves no one safe from critique, particularly Precious's mother, who is depicted as broken and then irrelevant in a novel that focuses on the protagonist's struggle to rebirth herself into existence. The scenes with Mary are layered with flooding of previous traumatic memories. When she stands at the sink during her second pregnancy, she remembers the previous labor and her mother's violence during it. This time, however, she will not tolerate the abuse: "My hand slip down in the dishwater, grab the butcher knife. She better not hit me, I ain' lyin'! If she hit me I will stab her ass to def, you hear me!" (13). The dynamic between them has shifted. As a teenager, the questioning, critical aspect of this developmental stage serves Precious well as she intends to defend herself. She will no longer scream "Mommy" as she is kicked. She is no longer a defenseless young child.

The social services system also fails to recognize the ugly reality of Mary Jones's abuse. As a character, Mary forces the reader to recognize structural and historical racism's ultimate damage. Although Precious tells the hospital workers the truth about Carl and instead of being removed from the home completely, she is left in Mary's care. In "Black 'Feminisms' and Pessimism: Abolishing Moynihan's Negro Family," Tiffany Lethabo King explains, "Precious as a literary figure represents the lives and experiences of a number of Black girls for whom the promise of safety within the confines of a respectable and heteronormative family has failed to materialize. The courage to create something new through unnaming something as true and universal in order to call forth another mode of living and thriving is the story that Precious and other survivors embody" (83). The maternal lineage is not biological but intentional in the classroom and through literature and found communities of survivors. In this way, it locates survival outside heteronormative views. If the Moynihan report privileged the nuclear family as the site of uplift, *Push* shatters that perspective and offers another queer perspective of chosen family. Mary blames Precious for stealing "her man," revealing that she privileges her own needs and concern with keeping that man and exposing an uncomfortable reality that contradicts the societal expectations about maternal care. Mary remains outside the range of redemption and becomes the embodiment of what Precious wants to shed to become fully herself. She does not exhibit the critical consciousness necessary to change her course and serves as a foil to Precious's questioning.

The system attempts to create a new Mary from Precious, and Precious battles the system as the moments when it attempts to place limits on her. This conflict appears most clearly when Precious encounters herself as a "file," with her entire life contained within a narrow schema organized without her input. Part of coming into her "literacy" that counters invisibility and traumatic dissociation includes reclaiming her "file"—the self that the system creates and reinforces through its "official" documentation. In an earlier reaction to "the file" occurs in a meeting with Ms. Lichenstein when Precious reacts angrily: "White cunt box got my file on her desk. I see it. I ain't late to lunch. Bitch knows how old I am" (7). Precious takes the file from the social worker in an effort to reclaim the power the file represents: "I know she writing reports on me. Reports go in file. File say what I could get, where I could go—if I get cut off, kicked out of Advancement House. Make me feel like Mama" (135). Precious wants out of the system and does not want her life managed by a stranger. Read aloud by Jermaine when Precious brings the file to her friends, the file blurs any portrait of Precious as a burgeoning writer who captures both mundane and horrific challenges in keen poetic turns: "In keeping with welfare reform I feel Precious would benefit from any of the various workfare programs in existence. Despite her obvious intellectual limitations, she is quite capable of working as a home attendant" (119). The social worker expects Precious to share her most painful memories in counseling sessions but fails to see Precious at all. She views Precious as a type. If Precious does not respond to her inquiries—since no trust has been built—Ms. Weiss interprets this reluctance as resulting from her "intellectual limitations" (119).

The report also appears critical of Ms. Rain's "emphasis on writing and reading books" (119). As an abuse survivor, Precious experiences this sense of objectification as retraumatizing. She seeks to gain control of her life without the interference that renders her helpless, even as the report reinscribes her as in a state of perpetual dependency: "The client seems to view the social service system and its proponents as her enemies, and yet while she mentions independent living, seems to envision social services, AFDC, as taking care of her forever" (120). Not only does she fail to acknowledge Precious's goals and hard work, but Ms. Weiss also condemns Precious with this stereotype. Precious's taking the file and bringing it into the Each One Teach One space as a text to analyze is an act of resistance to the tyranny of a system that refuses to view her complexity.

At another moment, Precious has a visceral reaction when she learns that the administrator/clerk at the alternative school has her file, and she experiences the file as an inescapable and deterministic rendering: "'They done sent my file! I almost spit, it make me so mad!'" (27). With her file comes the reductive view of her life, one that imposes meaning and restricts possibility: "I wonder what exactly do file say. I know it say I got a baby. Do it say who Daddy? What kinda baby? Do it say how pages the same for me, how much I weigh, fights I done had? I don't know what file say. I do know every time they wants to fuck wif me or decide something in my life, here they come wif the motherfucking file. Well, OK, they got file, know every mutherfucking thing. So what's the big deal, let's get it on" (28). Precious rebels against a system that often dehumanizes her and reduces her to another "at risk" Black girl in Harlem. Instead of support, these folders or files act as surveillance mechanisms that track her in the system but do little to support her growth and recovery.

With each encounter, she faces microaggressions that judge her surface without delving into her context or individual experience, such as when the social worker judges her place as a student: "'Sixteen is ahh rather ahh'—she clear her throat—*old* to still be in junior high school" (7). The counselor knows Precious's story and creates distance between them with her shaming inquiries. Precious attempts to regain agency and claim a sense of self: "I get up to go, Mrs Lichtenstein ax me to please sit down, she not through with me yet. But I'm through with her, thas what she don't get" (7), but she faces ridicule throughout the exchange with someone who should offer support: "This is your *second* baby?" she says. I wonder what else it say in that file with my name on it. I hate her" (8). The counselor shows no effort to reach Precious but continues to keep her at a comfortable distance with statements of fact delivered as moral judgments.

She suspends her for her pregnancy, which confirms that she is there to enforce the norms of respectability and not to care for the students as individuals: "You can't suspend me for being pregnant, I got rights!" (8). Mrs. Lichtenstein continues to exacerbate the situation by labeling Precious as uncooperative, and when Precious reacts by attempting to grab her to secure the file, Mrs. Lichtenstein calls for security. If Precious had not left the building, then a meeting with the school social worker would have ended with her in handcuffs as a pregnant teenager. She understands clearly the messages of contempt beneath the thin veneer of concern. "Concern" here was as if Precious was intentionally inconveniencing the school with her struggle.

Against these assaults on her dignity, Precious uses her poetic prowess with images and exposes the limitations through the system's representative. Even as Mrs. Lichenstein seeks to repair the damage from their previous exchange, she acts shocked when Precious informs her that she wants to return to math class: "She look at me like I want to suck a dog's dick or some shit" (7). She now believes that Precious, based on "Mr. Wicher says you're one of his best students, that you have an aptitude for math" (15). If that one conversation with Mr. Wicher had not happened behind the scenes, what would have happened? She expresses her frustration with her lack of agency here: "I was going to school everyday till her honky ass snatch me out the hall, fuck with my mind, make me go off on her, suspend me for school jus' because I am pregnant—you know, *end up* my education" (15). Rather than internalizing the extreme experiences, Precious crafts a language with which she can connect herself to others, particularly connecting the legacy provided by African American writers such as Langston Hughes and Alice Walker. Throughout the novel, she engages figurative language, demonstrating her facility with vivid imagery and poetic intuition, with some notable examples including, "My head is like the swimming pool at the Y on one-three-five. Summer full of bodies splashing, most in shallow end; one, two in deep end. Thas how all the time years is swimming in my head" (38) and "Everything seem like clothes in washing machine at laundry mat—round 'n round, up 'n down. One minute Mama's foot smashing into side of my head, next I'm jumping over desk on Mrs. Lichenstein's ass" (22). When she enters the Each One Teach One classroom for the first time, she also uses pool imagery to describe her experience: "My head is big 'lympic size pool, all the years, all the me's floating around glued shamed to desks while pee puddles get big near their feet" (40).

In another instance, she connects her familial trauma with the classroom and moves in between thinking about her previous school experience and the progression of abuse from her parents: "I stare at the blackboard pretending. I don't know what I'm pretending—that trains ain' riding through my head sometimes and that yes, I'm reading along with the class on page 55 of the reader" (39). When describing her cutting or self-mutilation, she searches for metaphors to approximate the experience: "I am a TV set wif no picture. I am broke wif no mind. No past or present time. Only the movies of being someone else" (112). Through her poetic language, she attempts to generate meaning and to name an often intangible, dissociative feeling, a gesture that trauma theorists have explored when considering the limits of the literal in expressing survivor aftermath.

In *Push*, we see the transformation of the body from a site of pain to a site of potentiality and promise through the merging of childrearing and literacy as Precious learns self-care and finds inspiration in her relationship to her child. As Marlo D. David observes: "*The Color Purple* and *Push* . . . stand out for the way that they propose print literacy—reading and writing—as a viable means to challenge and critique hegemonic ideas about black motherhood as well as black women's capacity for social and political citizenship" (199). Poetry is often linked to Abdul, such as when she chooses to memorize Langston Hughes's "Mother to Son" for the class, a poem that involves a mother bearing witness to her own life in an address to her son. Her letters to Ms. Rain also begin as poetry and include her struggle with the possibility of losing to the disease.

Both Elizabeth Donaldson and Wendy Roundtree note the connections of *Push* within the larger African American literary tradition and look particularly at the connections to previously sexual abuse survivors in Toni Morrison's *Bluest Eye* and Alice Walker's *Color Purple*. Roundtree extends this connection to demonstrate how Precious employs tools of language for her own purposes. Roundtree explains, "By having Precious use other people's words from everyday speech, addresses, and literature to aid her in expressing her blues, Sapphire['s] intertextuality creates hybridized text, and thereby, verbally connects Precious to other African American experiences" (142). Precious enters the community Baldwin describes in his letter to Hansberry noted in the first chapter on *Johnnas*, and she marks it specifically her own, changing it and creating a new text by incorporating voices from her own experience.

Her developing literacy in writing and reading also provides an alphabet to bring her dissociation to her awareness. As she tries to formulate words and decipher the page, she also puts into words her experience with dissociation. However, she also floats away as she struggles to make sense of words since learning to read involves a vulnerability that returns her to a crisis state. Precious questions Ms. Rain and her ideas about daily writing: "How we gonna write if we can't read? Shit, how we gonna write if we can't write! I don't remember never doing no writing before. My head spinning I'm scared maybe we, maybe this ain' class for me" (49).

The students step up to the board and begin to write the alphabet. Rita cries. It is an emotional space, this "beginning" with a "single step." Again, she encounters her body's response to stress, and academic performance triggers trauma response with flooding: "All the air go out my body. I grab my stomach. Ms. Rain look scared." She becomes flooded and panics. In her panic "I see

TVS I hear rap music I want something to eat I want fuck feeling from Daddy I want die I want die" (53). She is experiencing a posttraumatic flooding and wants to ground herself to return to her body and gain control but then despises herself for these desperate impulses.

The panic occurs when she needs to face that "the pages look alike": "I say 'A Day at the Beach.' She says very good and closes the book. I want to cry. I want to laugh. I want to hug kiss Ms. Rain. She make me feel good. I never readed nuffin' before" (55). She becomes overcome with the intensity of her bodily response: "This gonna end, even if it end by me stop breathing. Thas what I want sometimes. Sometime I hurt so bad I want to not wake up, want breathing to stop in my sleep. Have me *don't* wake up. Other times I start to go a huh a huh ahuh ahuh AHUH A HUH and I grab my chess 'cause I can't breathe, then I WANT breathin' bad" (57). The memories of the abuse flood her more frequently during her pregnancy since her condition provides a constant reminder of the rape. The school change and her mother's reaction to it also evoke a stress response.

For Precious, language offers stability, even though the stress related to school and the classroom reading can overwhelm her into a flashback at times. When dealing with her mother's requests for food, Precious recites the alphabet in her head to help her cope. The alphabet often serves as an anchor and as part of her developing emotional literacy while she navigates her relationship with Mary, who has not left the house in years and relies on public assistance as the "caregiver" to her daughter and granddaughter (who does not live with her). She cannot return to any healthy state without acknowledging the harm she has done to her child and herself. Precious recognizes that her mother will never see her as a daughter requiring care and respect for her development. It is too late for their relationship, despite the efforts of the social worker to attempt a reconciliation. Precious dreams about rescuing herself: "I look at little Precious and big Mama and feel hit feeling, feel like killing

Mama. But I don't, instead I call little Precious and say, Come to Mama but I means me. Come to *me* little Precious. Little Precious look at me, smile, and start to sing: ABCDEFG ..." (59). She has the opportunity to return to herself at the age of seven when the abuse started, and her education suffered, and retrieve the child from the abusive mother.

To support this emotional, creative, and intellectual development, Ms. Rain promotes an environment of radical self-acceptance that leads to self-love and actualization. When one of the girls, Jo Ann, tries to create distance between herself and the other girls, Ms. Rain holds her accountable for an honest self-assessment (59). Precious sees the wisdom in Ms. Rain's approach, although Jo Ann is angry for now: "I see what she doing, I think. Jo Ann tryin' to act like she ain' one of us. Ms. Rain tryin' to git her to 'cept herself for where she at. She ain' no G.E.D. girl, leas' not yet" (59). When Ms. Rain indicates that they will "'figure out what we gonna do here'" (42), she opens up a space for self-determination and participation in the classroom agenda for the students. These inclusive gestures, including the desk circle as a pedagogical strategy to diminish hierarchy, surprise Precious initially and stir discomfort: "Everybody looking at me now. In circle I see everybody, everybody see me. I wish for back of the class again for a second, then think never that again. I kill myself first 'fore I let that happen" (46). The space of the classroom is significant. It is connected also with level of participation and with visibility. Precious may not understand the context of the lesson due to her struggles with reading, but she is no longer hiding in the classroom or attempting to shrink or minimize her presence. For Precious, there is a need to be in an educational environment that sees her and includes other young women who have faced considerable adversity in their short lives. Their life experience can be integrated into their learning, and there is a way that they see themselves reflected in each other and the progress and setbacks made in the process.

In this context, Precious allows herself to become vulnerable, moving away from the dissociative strategies by which her body and mind involuntarily shut down. She reflects as she processes this change: "Ms. Rain look at me. I'm the only one haven't spoken. I wanna say something but don't know how. I'm not used to talkin', how can I say it?" (48). Precious acknowledges clearly her deep desire to feel seen and to move behind coping skills that no longer serve her and her development as a student: "I want to tell her what I always wanted to tell someone, that the pages, 'cept for the ones with pictures, look all the same to me; the back row I'm not in today; how I sit in a chair seven years old all day wifout moving. But I'm not seven years old. But I am crying. I look Ms. Rain in the face, tears is coming down my eyes, but I am not sad or embarrass" (48). When she asks for validation that she belongs, Ms. Rain provides a clear affirmation. The emotional vulnerability and inner strength required in this moment makes clear that Precious has a core reserve. She is somehow brilliantly clear from the defensiveness that may have undermined her ability to receive what she needed. Precious demonstrates a kind of genius of emotional literacy. With all of the obvious signs of "at risk" and abjectness, she has at her command a nuanced emotional vocabulary and insight that suggests her giftedness.

Ms. Rain encourages them to write from the beginning, translating their inner thoughts as best they can phonetically on the page for her to respond and draw out additional thinking. The journaling allows the students to remain present and to bridge their inner worlds—often distractions that may overwhelm and cause a disconnect as they try to stay engaged in the classroom. The excitement and positive stress of learning new material or skills may be experienced as threatening in the mixed signaling of posttraumatic experience. The first sentence she writes in class refers directly to her child: "li Mg o mi m (Little Mongo on my mind)" (61). After Ms. Rain writes out the spelling corrections, Precious makes the changes: "I copy Little Mongo's name from where

Ms. Rain had wrote it" (61). For the first time in the classroom or perhaps any public space, Precious has put her connection to her child in writing and committed it to the page. In the earlier moment of her life, when the nurse collects the information for the birth certificate and realizes that Precious's newborn came from incestuous rape, their connection as mother and child is marked by shame and the grief of the nurse, who serves as a witness to the painful reality.

Now Precious can articulate her connection to her child before a different kind of witness, Ms. Rain, who supports Precious through her journey toward a new self-in-the-world: "Ms. Rain read, 'Little Mongo is my child?' She have a question in her voice. I say, 'Yes yes.' Ms. Rain know Little Mongo is my child 'cause I wrote it in my journal. I am happy to be writing. I am happy to be in school. Ms. Rain say we gonna write everyday, that means home too. 'N she gonna write back too. 'N she gonna write back everyday. Thas great" (62). She uses the alphabet to ground her when she begins to uncover her feelings about the abuse. Or the recitation of the alphabet allows her to put her previous trauma into a language that names it as abuse and recognizes her vulnerability as a child. While imagining how she will read to her new baby, she enacts the way she wishes her mother had responded to the father's abuse: "Can't you see Precious is a beautiful chile like white chile in magazines or on toilet paper wrappers. Precious is a blue-eye skinny chile whose hair is long braids.... Git off Precious, fool!" (66). She assesses her actual value to her mother and recognizes it as contingent on the welfare check. Precious plans her future with her child and speaks the letters of the alphabet so the baby can hear while she writes them down in her journal. She indicates an association with each letter, allowing her to develop a literacy that connects to her life: "Listen baby, Muver love you. Muver not dumb." After reciting the alphabet again, she tells her baby: "Thas the alphabet. Twenty-six letters in all. Them letters make up words. Them words everything" (67). Even the naming of her child provides her with purpose and power. Abdul, "servant of god," which she learned from a book of African names. She also recognizes the value inherent in her own name—Precious: "I am Precious ABDC . . . / My baby is born / My baby is black / I am girl / I am black / I want a house to live" (76). Her identity emerges in deep connection to her ability to name and to explore her world in language.

In addition to witnessing the reactions of others to understand the abuse, Precious also pieces together bits of information from Louis Farrakhan and his lectures on rape and other forms of exploitation during slavery and through its legacy. Her first pregnancy was when she was twelve, and she was not truly aware of it. She went into labor and had the baby on the kitchen floor with her mother beating her. She had no prenatal care. Pregnancy continued to be a point of shame due to her age and the incest. Once she enters the Each One Teach One space, she allows herself to become aware of her body: "I don't pretend I'm not pregnant no more. I let it above my neck, in my head" (63). The classroom community expresses concern over the lack of prenatal care she has received. For once, she has some genuine support and can begin to connect with her experience. Part of reconnecting to herself involves sorting through her feelings about her newborn child. She acknowledges the deep conflict she experiences in loving a child who reminds her of rape and who also threatens her progress at school. However, when Ms. Rain tries to convince her to give Abdul up for adoption, Precious cannot abide. She loves her child as part of her healing because she recognizes her own innocence when she acknowledges his.

The exchange she has with Ms. Rain in the journal reveals a young woman who can sort through the painful complexities of her situation, including the ways that the many adults have failed to support her effectively and respect her agency. Even as Ms. Rain asks about her grandmother's neglect in an effort to steer Precious away from privileging the grandmother's desire to keep the children, Precious continues to associate the children with herself, her vulnerability, and her need for someone not to abandon her. She has been forced to give enough of herself away, and the thought of losing more is unbearable. The exchange becomes more impassioned as Precious's determination to keep her children becomes clear. She develops cognitive strategies to chase away negative thoughts: "What I gonna be, queen of babies? No, I gonna be queen of those ABCs—readin' 'n writin.' I'm not going to stop going to school 'n I not going to give Abdul up and I is gonna get Little Mongo back one day" (75). Even in the direst circumstances, Precious has learned a core resilience, anchored to her love of learning and language, that centers her: "Help me. One thing from going to school 'n talking in class I done learned to talk up" (76).

Ms. Rain connects the lessons in school to their lives and to justice issues. In the classroom, Ms. Rain opens up space for reflection on policy and cultural topics that affect their lives directly. When Precious reads her file and discovers that Ms. Weiss intends to recommend her for a low-skilled job in the welfare-to-work program, the prompt for the morning journaling includes "Workfare and education" (120). The young women gain literacy and voice in relation to the culture wars. They recognize that they have long been at the center of these heated political debates and that their lives have been represented flatly and without nuance. They create their own public space in which to raise their views about topics in the spirit of "nothing about us without us." Precious does the calculations and recognizes that this system will exploit her labor and leave her with no time to spend with her child. It is a family-hostile program that will leave her with no opportunity for growth.

Precious describes her teacher's work—"to reprogram us to love ourselves. I love me" (76)—and the benefits of radical love that has strengthened her insights into both her creativity and the forces that threaten to contain it. Precious's new life includes literary references that support her writing and her life. She discovers the civil rights movement through her class reading: "I ain' know black people in this country went through shit like that" (82). She stays at the Langston Hughes house overnight while she waits for her bed at Advancement House in Harlem and notes its significance: "Me and Abdul in the Dream Keeper's house!"(80). Once she settles into her new space at Advancement House, she has a bookshelf with selections that speak to her experience in some way, such as *Pat King's Family*, a book for new adult readers with a story about a single mother who must fend for herself and her children after her husband abandons them, and *The Life of Lucy Fern*, which opens with thirteen-year-old Ruth Ferm, about to give birth to a child, and she has told no one about the pregnancy. Precious's books also include *A Piece of Mine*, a short story collection with Black women as the central characters, which Alice Walker promoted in the 1980s. She reads *The Color Purple* in class and responds with intense emotion. The class discussion of the book and Ms. Rain's self-identification as a lesbian opens up Precious's views and causes her to rethink her reliance on Farrakhan. She has found another path to a liberation consciousness: "Things going good in my life, almost like *The Color Purple*.... I love *The Color Purple*, that book give me so much strength" (82–83). She has discussions with Ms. Rain about the politics of representation and the protesting against Alice Walker's depiction of Black men. In their discussions of the novel, Precious analyzes with a writerly perspective, responding to the criticism that the Walker novel received for its "fairytale ending": "I would say, well shit like that can be true. Life can work out for the best sometimes. Ms. Rain love *Color Purple* too but say realism has its virtues too. Izm, smsm! Sometimes I wanna tell Ms. Rain to shut up with all the IZM stuff" (83).

Precious wants to dwell in the possibility that life holds hope, that the narrative of realism has its limitations in that the ceiling may begin to threaten the outlook for people struggling in the present. This attitude reflects Precious's continual search for beauty and specialness, such as her connections to celebrity and pop culture when she is abused. Precious learns about halfway houses and battered women's experience through reading memoirs and novels: "They tell her, You is 1/2way between the life you had and the life you want to have. Ain't that nice. You should read that book if you have a chance" (83–84). In this moment, Precious addresses her audience directly, a gesture that indicates that she recognizes her role in shaping and sharing her narrative. She describes herself as on a "threshold" and looking into the future when her mother returns to her life to disrupt this peace of mind with the news about Carl's HIV status. The boundaries between life and fiction arise when Precious hopes that—at the very least—Carl is not her biological father, and that like Celie, she can be spared the pain of incest. However, reality does not spare Precious the ugly truth.

As she opens up to the possibility her relationship with creativity offers, she finds herself naming the experience, revealing her facility with poetic language and her developing emotional literacy that will help her self-regulate, such as when she hears a song playing in the background to her distress upon learning about her AIDS exposure: "Song caught on me like plastic bags on tree branches" (87). The song threatens to overwhelm her as she imagines a chase scene with Adbul. "Where is my *Color Purple*?" (87), she asks herself and continues to narrate the experience: "I listen to song, I can hear it now. It's Aretha." She hears Aretha Franklin's *Angel* as a gift that names her for an angel, someone to rescue her from her pain. Even as she finds love and a purpose to persevere through her relationship with Abdul, she now must face whether her young child has HIV as well. In a moment that appears unbearable, Precious finds strength in her literacy award: "That is good proof to me that I can do anything" (88). Her inner monologue includes desperate questioning cushioned by statements of promise: "Mr Wicher say I got aptitude for maff" (88) as Precious engages in cognitive strategies to buoy her against the overwhelming emotions. She settles herself with the practical demands of motherhood: "I gotta go upstairs to the nursery to get Abdul. I think about this later. It make me feel stupid crazy, I mean stupid crazy" (89). Precious gains emotional literacy and self-regulation that she has taught herself, with the support of her Each One Teach One experience of course, but the baseline gift was already there.

In her exchange with Ms. Rain during the class after she learns about the HIV exposure, she continues to express her emotions in all their complexity. The initial entry contains her gratitude and her hopes. She tells Ms. Rain that she loves her and shares her aspirations for a career in computers and an independent life with her children, but ends in "why Me?" In her follow-up response, she writes a poem: "Blu Ran / Blue RAIN / Rain / is gr___(*gray*) / but saty (*stay*) / my rain" and identifies herself as "Precious Jones / the poet" (90). Even in her despair, she claims this identity and understands the power of self-definition. In this moment when the fear of an early death threatens to rob her of all hope, she names herself as a poet, as a creative being who will tell her own story. She continues to communicate through her painful process of coming to terms with the testing and her HIV status. In her poems, she connects Alice Walker with the prayer that she offers.

Her desire to present her experience drives her to search for more words, for a greater fluency: "I gotta learn more than ABCs now. I got to learn more than read write, this big BIG" (93). Discovering her HIV-positive status does not shut her down; rather, it compels her to write as a lifeline. The class assignment to compose a life story aligns with her need to record her experience: "From the girls who been here awhile I only one ain' done my story yet" (95) and addresses her reader again: "When I have time I read you what the other girls wrote" (95). The other stories provide perspective and speak to the power of narrative to counter isolation and abjection: "These girlz is my friends" (95), and "They and Ms Rain is my friends and family" (95). Precious reflects on the solidarity and creativity that will push her through this painful moment. When she feels overwhelmed: "I say I drownin' in a river," Ms. Rain compels her forward: "Writing could be the boat carry you to the other side." Even if she is tired and resists the writing, Ms. Rain tells her to tap into her connection to language: "'Precious, you gotta push.' And I do" (97). In her depression, her language changes and her spelling breaks down: "whut i got to remember i nevr dun forgit" (100), but she can write herself back into a place of gratitude and positivity.

Precious thinks, grieves, and loves in poetry, even as she expresses her connection to Abdul, who "was a dark spot in the sky; then turn to life in me" (95). "He song in my life . . . the voice of love say, Mama" (96). She begins to form a more womanist consciousness that celebrates Blackness and even asks herself about Abdul's future as a man: "When he grow up he gonna laff big black girls? He gon' laff at dark skin like he got? One thing I say about Farrakhan and Alice Walker they help me like being black" (96). The class reads Audre Lorde during this crisis point in Precious's life, and she reflects on its appeal: "What is a black unicorn? I don't really understand the poem but I like it" (96). Her poetry develops to incorporate the beauty in Harlem, "not jazzee / Harlem /of Langston Hughes . . . this / a Harlem done / took / a beating" (103) but with a "sky opn / blu legs / for / sun" (104). She writes about the vacant lot on 124th Street in a poem that focuses on filth and ugliness: "I HATE / HATE / UGLY" (105). The drug addicts have eyes "like far away space ships" (105). Precious captures her surroundings in poetic language and sees herself in the role: "I think about being a poet or rapper or an artist even" (109). The art she observes and values now appears organically to transform sites of abandonment. Precious uses the transformation she witnesses to form her own aesthetic, and she writes poems about the garbage and despair in vacant lots and appreciates the murals that allow beauty to appear in unexpected spaces: "It's this guy on one-two-five, Franco, he done painted pictures on the steel gates that's over almos' all the store windows. At night you walk down and each one is painted different. I like that better than a museum" (109). Pleasure and promise exist in her newfound vision in both the mundane and the imaginary, and she captures her journey: "I am homer on a voyage / but from our red bricks in piles / of usta be buildings / and windows of black / broke glass eyes" (127). Waiting to include her story in the class book, she spends her time cultivating this vision, the mark of her new identity as a writer, carefully crafting her narrative.

Push offers significant insight into the way the academic space must acknowledge and navigate trauma. The students and Ms. Rain deep clean and decorate the space with objects significant to them. They share a sense of ownership and belonging that fosters the healing connection essential to learning. Precious reflects on her educational journey and its ability to ground her in the present to counter the dysregulation that she felt previously: "Me, I, just look at the sun coming in through the front window. Pretty soon it move around and around and come in through the side window. I like the routine of school, the dream of school. I wonder where I be if I had been learning all those years at I.S. 146" (107). Tom Brunzell, Lea Waters, and Helen Stokes address the possibilities for trauma-informed classrooms, which suggests the classroom created by Ms. Rain: "The current landscape of trauma-informed practice for primary and secondary classrooms has focused on teaching practices that seek to repair emotional dysregulation and fix broken attachment," (3) and "when teachers focus on repairing regulatory competencies and maladaptive attachment styles together with a positive education approach, the resulting pedagogy is a full-bodied approach where teachers can envision their classroom as a therapeutic milieu addressing the effects of adverse childhood experiences and structuring trajectory-shifting learning to enable posttraumatic growth, psychological wellbeing, and academic aspirations for their students" (6). Precious's new experience fosters a sense of hope and an orientation toward the possible: "I think about my future a lot. I think a lot. All the time.

Ms. Rain say I am intellectually alive and curious. I am just trying to figure out what is going on out here. How what happen to me could happen in modern days. I guess I am still trying to figure out just what *has* happen to me" (124). The struggle with visibility is named clearly as the desire to be seen from within: "And if they could see *inside* me they would see something lovely and not keep laughing at me, throwing spitballs . . . But I am not different on the inside. Inside I thought was so beautiful is a black girl too" (125). Through her writing she questions the failures of the system that will limit her future but did nothing to bring justice to her when she needed it most as a twelve-year-old girl pregnant by her father.

Her poetry expresses the anger at class privilege that will leave her as a caregiver to a wealthy white woman. After stating clearly: "I kill 'em first," she moved into the opening line from Blake's Tyger poem, followed by "That's what's in Precious / Jones heart—a tyger" (128). A fighter with fierce resolve and astute cultural observation, she likens the girls and herself to "bombs" awaiting detaination when the memories emerge: "Everything is floating around me now. Like geeses from the lakes. I see wings beating beating hear geeses. It's more birds than geeses . . . I see flying. Feel flying. *Am* flying. Far up, but my body down in circle" (129). Precious's creativity has resulted in a poetic flight and freedom in which she manages her posttraumatic symptoms in the container of images, so she remains able to engage with the present meaningfully with the help of Rita's holding her hand. After the meeting, she returns to her bird imagery: "I'm alive inside. A bird is my heart. Mamma and Daddy is not win. I'm winning" (131).

In Ms. Weiss's office during the confrontation with Mary about the abuse, Precious sees clearly how compromised her mother is: "Umm hmm, I was raised by a psycho maniac fool" (135). There is no connection between them. She refused to share her writing and cites Ms. Rain's protocol for choice and autonomy in relation to the journal writing. Why would she share? A small gesture of kindness from the house mother moves her to consider her desires: "I think how *alive* I am . . . I got poems, a son, friends" (137). Her mother reminds her of death and disease, which she resists: "Everybody know I write poems. People respect me" (118). The final moments of her narrative revolve around a moment with Abdul: "I love to hold him on my lap, open up the world to him" . . . In his beauty I see my own" (139-40). The novel ends with an affirmation of narrative when she reads to her child: "Want me to stop daydreaming and read him a story before nap time. I do" (140). In choosing to mother Abdul well, Precious defines her own worth and values through connection, a Black mother and child, future uncertain, yet complete in their relation to each other. Precious will not abandon herself and will instead continue to write herself into a new existence. Precious's poems of daily life frame the life stories of her classmates in the Each One Teach One collection at the end of *Push*. She has chosen not to write a conventional narrative but instead to represent her voice in poetry: "I can see / I can read / nobody can see now / but I might be a poet, rapper, I got / water colors." Precious articulates herself into the heart of the poem: "Ms Rain say / walk on / go into the poem / the HEART of it / beating / like / a clock / a virus / tick / tock." In the poem that closes *Push*, Precious returns to her mentors Alice Walker and Langston Hughes and exposes the connection between the forsaken urban landscape in the post-civil rights era and the restrictions on her individual freedom. Although she has found hope in her poetry, Precious ends with uncertainty. The novel pushes against neoliberal impulse at the end when Precious connects her freedom and the limitations on it to the larger context when she finds hope in connection and nontraditional chosen family but resists a neat resolution.

Robin M. Boylorn addresses these concerns of focusing only on strength and resolve in "Unbreakable, or the Problem with Praising Blackgirl Strength": "Blackgirls are not unbreakable. There has to be a way to protect our Jadas, our Ambers, and ourselves without shaming and silencing our visceral responses to trauma. There has to be a way to be okay without having to be so damn strong. We have to make room for Blackgirl emotional fluidity. We have to make room for sadness, for anger, for hysteria. We can raise a fist in the air with tears in our eyes and still be powerful." This call for a recognition of the fullness of experience is echoed powerfully in the spoken word poem "Sandra Bland" about the 2015 reported suicide of the young activist while jailed after a violent encounter with an aggressive police officer during a traffic stop. In the poem, Kai Davis, Nayo Jones, and Jasmine Combs ask, "What if that night, her voice was a ceasefire," and "What if she laid down her arms and walked into the light before they could drag her? A final act of protest. What if she wasn't the hero smiling in every picture? Does that make her any less deserving of a revolution?" The poem demonstrates clearly the witness performed by the poets to another Black woman's life and death and creates poetry from the complexity denied Sandra Bland in debates that threaten to flatten her full humanity. In "'Artists without Art Form': A Look at One Black Woman's World of Unrevered Black Women" Renita Weems offers a critique and a witness for the creative efforts that seek to value this complexity, in the way that Precious and her classroom community validated each other while entering into a language to express their lives:

> Over the years the Black woman novelist has not been seriously. "Shallow," "emotional," "unstructured," "reactionary," "just too painful," are just some of the criticisms made of her work. That she is a woman makes her work marginal. That she is Black makes it minor. That she is both makes it alien. But these criticisms have not stopped the flow of her ink. The Black woman writer has insisted on portraying the tragic and fortunate of her lot.... The Black woman artist will revere the Black woman. For it is her duty to record and capture with song, clay, strings, dance and, in this case, ink, the joys and pains of Black womanhood. And the person who is sane, secure, and sensitive enough to revere her art is the same person who will revere her life. (94)

For Precious, resiliency is connected to literacy and creativity, and through this growth, she is able to "read" her struggle within the larger structural framework and in a collective space. However, it would be a mistake to align Precious's resiliency through creativity with the absolute strength, which is also a posttraumatic restriction of emotional range. Via writing and reading and literary expression, she seeks avenues to contain the flooding that may overwhelm while also finding the freedom to explore her emotional range. In her daily poetry, she engages in divergent thinking—creative thinking—that is expansive and risky in that it moves away from comfortable retreat or withdrawal. Poetry is not a luxury for Precious, not an earned reward, but a way to live. Within the space of poetry, even in its ambiguity and fragile certainty, she is "HERE."

CHAPTER 4

"MY BODY OF A FREE BOY . . . MY BODY OF DANCE"

Violence and the Choreography of Survival in Sapphire's *The Kid*

The Kid, Sapphire's long-awaited second novel, delivers a decisive blow to Precious Jones's story of redemption and the vicarious uplift offered to its readers. Readers found a powerful hope in *Push* and invested in her journey from serial abuse and illiteracy, witnessing the profound grace she receives in her role as Abdul's mother. *The Kid* tests the limits of this hope when we must come to terms with Abdul's life as a young, gifted, and Black AIDS orphan. Interweaving social-political commentary with the intertextuality of cultural sources from visual arts, dance, and literature, at its core *The Kid* is a posttraumatic counternarrative of an orphaned artist. Perhaps most striking and brilliant—if potentially misunderstood by critics and readers alike—is Sapphire's commitment to risk alienating her audience's ability to identify with her protagonist's response to trauma. In an interview, Sapphire asserts, "He's very close to my heart—I love this boy," yet she has written a character who abuses himself and others, including young children, while attempting to manage his own traumatic history (Martin). *The Kid* asks its readers to consider their response to a child whose story navigates the violence of extreme marginalization and sexual exploitation, even when that child acts out in horrifying ways in order to survive and fails to sustain a lasting human connection. The novel challenges us to witness a young artist's development as he negotiates creativity and expression with degradation and terror. This essay argues that Sapphire's *The Kid* offers a necessary intervention against "good-victim" paradigms, particularly as they limit our capacity to witness the reoccurring trauma of young Black men whose bodies remain overdetermined as threatening within the dominant cultural script. This intervention involves a disentanglement from Abdul's literary precursor, his mother, to unmoor the survival narrative. This rupture leaves him adrift and estranged, creating a free-floating signifier that faces repeated efforts to erase the boundaries of individual identity, until he dances. Only in the moment, only unanchored from connection to past and future, can Abdul choreograph an autonomous self, find a rhythm to counter the ruptures, and create a cohesive present in which he contains the dissolving stability he encounters once he stops dancing.

The novel's epigraph from Flannery O'Connor suggests Abdul's complete unmooring as both a son and a literary figure associated with his mother's legacy: "Where you come from is gone, where you thought you were going to never was there, and where you are is no good unless you can get away from it." These words speak to the novel's unsentimental treatment of family history and genealogy and Abdul's perpetual flight from his current conditions. An orphan and an artistic soul, Abdul is both bereft and free from the restraint of connection. Throughout the novel, uncovering hidden truths does not provide solace or sustenance. Abdul's journey involves a disconcerting mix of erasure of self and fragmented visibility, although ultimately, he finds self-creation through dance. *The Kid* begins with a mother's death and funeral and the end of a relationship with one of the late twentieth century's most compelling and controversial fictional characters, who evoked complex responses from readers and critics alike. As a literary figure, Precious came to represent the rise of the abject and the power of literacy to help survivors overcome extreme trauma and the limitations of poverty, even as her portrayal raised questions about stereotypes and sensationalism in contemporary literature. With the death of Precious, the reader has lost the uplift associated with her powerful story. Indeed, her death and Abdul's subsequent destitution feel like a betrayal. We see now that her story's end is perhaps different than many readers had hoped for and imagined possible. Her death represents the end of certain expectations in relation to this positive trajectory in its most direct terms. During her journey, Precious struggles with feeling invisible, and she raises her child in his early years with a clear sense that he has a place at the table and is recognized for his unique value. For example, in *Push*, Precious describes her experiences with feeling invisible, particularly when faced with academic testing, and compares herself to a movie scene when vampires do not show up in an instant photograph and "when you get right down to it they don't exist" (31). In *The Kid*, we meet a child whose first nine years have been characterized by care and nurturing. Abdul's journey assumes the opposite trajectory, and he moves from his place as a child at the center of his mother's universe to someone who becomes completely lost in the system that repeatedly attempts to eradicate his claim to a stable public and private identity. His mother offers him a borrowed gift, in the sense that she can never provide the security to see it develop to fruition. "Wake up, little man" (3), Rita nudges, suggesting the radical turn on which his reality verges, as Abdul dreams of his mother's birthday, in contrast to the funeral he will soon attend. A woman within his dreams bears a gift but surprises him with rotten teeth, signaling perhaps his relationship to maternal nurturing from a terminally ill source (3). An immediate and sharp contrast emerges between imagination's role in resilience and escape and the wake-up-to-reality moment. Abdul's inner world will continue to return to a creative impulse that drives him forward when faced with extreme threats from the outer world.

From the beginning, we see a child who has been taught to question and who is confident in his intelligence. Abdul's early life included frequent cultural expeditions, and his nine-year-old thoughts lead repeatedly to the sense that he could travel—explore—within the safety of his connection to his mother. Precious composes a childhood for Abdul with a mixture of elements to fortify political awareness, cultural literacy, traditional academics, and personal responsibility. Unlike Precious's upbringing, in which she was repeatedly demoralized and abused emotionally and physically, Abdul benefits from his mother's fierce determination for her child to see the connections between self and community. He has internalized the voice of his mother and her sense of accountability and personal power, for example, when he reflects: "When I go to put the foil in the trash can, it falls onto the sidewalk 'cause the can is so full. Oh well, I tried," and he hears his mother's voice in his mind telling him: "You gotta do more than try! You gotta do it! I pick the foil up and put it on top of the heap of trash in the can" (10). She also reminds him: "Just remember your private parts are yours an' no one is supposed to touch 'em 'less you say so, hear? Hear?" (8–9). Her words demonstrate the responsible parent acknowledging the possible risks her child may face without her. Precious has provided Abdul with the kind of instruction most parents hope will empower their children. Soon after we meet him, we can look back at this moment with bitter sadness since Abdul will not be able to heed this advice and will have very little physical agency or choice within his new environments. Perhaps the foundational sense that his body belongs to him—something many victims of childhood sexual abuse, including the young Precious, do not have—allows for some resiliency when he becomes a victim. We do see in the aftermath that he directs the blame away from himself once he leaves the abusive environment of foster care, which may be essential for his ultimate survival. Abdul had access to information early on and was encouraged to understand himself and see himself as someone with agency. He does not have a home environment that would expose him to the dangerous possibility of internalizing shame.

Part of his upbringing prior to his mother's death involved remaining innocent about his mother's past, and his meeting with Blue Rain provides some insight into Precious's true story of abuse, AIDS, and illiteracy, about which Abdul knew nothing. From this encounter, we witness his precarious relationship with his family history, individual identity, and memory. Blue Rain emphasizes Precious's legacy when she urges Abdul to understand "what a good game you can still play when the deck is stacked against you" (17). He is then informed that he needs to go to a foster home in the morning, news to which he reacts by vomiting into a garbage can. We get a view of this radical disruption from a child's perspective. Everything Abdul has ever known is behind him, and the access is swiftly sealed from him via coffins, padlocked apartment doors, and state child services protocol. His world as he has known it is gone, yet he goes through a painful inventory of the items that are left behind, material objects imbued with the memories of an orderly life:

> My suit is on the bed folded up and wrapped in plastic from the dry cleaners, my shirt too. My shirt, black suit, good shoes, and leather jacket, and what I got on—jeans, my Batman T-shirt, and sneakers is all I got from home. Everything else I got is at home. My CD player, my mother's but I'm the one use it most, my TV, my mother's but she don't like TV, my computer, my mother's but my school don't have computers for the fourth grade, my jeans, not baggies, my mother don't allow that, my down jacket Triple Phat, Timberland boots, my favorites, what I'm gonna wear when it gets cold. My swimming trunks for when I go swimming, flippers, guy down the hall gave me, even though I can't swim yet. My CDs, me and my mother's, some is mine, some is hers. All is hers, she said after I traded one I thought

was mine, MC Lyte, for Biggie Smalls. My mother attaches to old school. My G.I. Joe men, Indians, Crazy Horse, Red Cloud, Custard and the soldiers, map from the Battle of the Little Bighorn, marbles (I never play with), string, knife (Swiss Army knife that I'm never, NEVER spozed to take out the house), the goldfish, they probably not alive anymore if didn't no one go in and feed 'em. My books. I got a lot of books about black people and Indians. I like Native Americans better than black people. Ain't no Indians stupid like Danny. My play clothes, crayons, paints, my paints but my mother use 'em more than me. On my dresser is a picture of my mom, where's it at? Who got my stuff? I want it. (25–26)

This detailed inventory is set again in another memory to which he returns as he processes his loss, which involves the story of a young child named Tyrese who is kidnapped by his brother's gang rivals. On the television news, he hears reports of the child's fingers found in a bag at the local McDonalds. Precious attempts to reassure him: "Nothing like that is ever going to happen to you. You and Tyrese are two different people" (30). This story allows Abdul to understand a child's ultimate vulnerability, although his mother attempts to assuage his fears and potential identification with the victim. After the loss of his mother, his efforts to create lists, to conjure wholeness from parts of a former life are attempts to counter the forces that incinerate and scatter the remains of a once-secure life. What will his late mother's reassurances mean now that he is faced with his new circumstances? No one stands between him and these dangers now. This moment clearly foreshadows the vulnerability of children, whose bodies become pawns and whose identities as individuals become erased.

In *The Kid*, many people recognize Abdul's gifts, yet he loses his "official identity." The people around him recognize him mainly in relation to their desire or needs. Once he enters foster care, violence becomes a constant presence in Abdul's life. The physical and sexual abuse compound the threats to his identity. *The Kid* reinforces a clear, undeniable connection between violence and vulnerability. Poor and orphaned children, particularly boys of color, fall under the collective radar and face dire circumstances because of their invisible status. To exacerbate this struggle with marginalization, traumatic experience undermines one's sense of self in the world and forces the recognition of the permeability of the psychic self. It pierces the membrane of a secure self and shatters the symbolic order anchoring meaning. There is a way that one could read his experience as representative of the African American experience, an allegorical rendering of disruption from origins followed by institutionalized exploitation. In Abdul's case, he loses connection with the mother who values him and who provides a sense of origins and connection to something much larger than his individual life. On both social and individual levels, Abdul's identity is traumatized, yet throughout *The Kid*, he exhibits signs of agency and resiliency due to his mother's early work and his powerful imagination.

A discernible gesture to eradicate the child's former self occurs when Abdul walks through the door of his first foster home, and he becomes J. J. to his new foster mother. The loss of name accompanies a general contempt that shocks him initially: "I look up at her. Why is she talking to me like that?" (32). This shock underscores that he has experienced himself as a person with some value and has not known this kind of address. His new foster mother disabuses him quickly of the notion that his previous value holds meaning in this current context:

> "J. J., you just like all the rest come in here, you got to adjust. Whatever you had at home is over and probably never was! I know how you kids make shit up." She opens my envelope, looks in a folder, and starts reading, "'Father unknown, mother deceased November 1, 1997, HIV-related illness.' Uh huh just what I thought, so OK, J. J., relax, you like everybody else here." She looks in the drawer. "Is that a suit?" (34).

The moment stands in stark contrast to Abdul's previous inventory, with this list corresponding to an effort to diminish his sense of value and ownership over his life.

Later in his journey, when placed in a Catholic boy's home, Abdul acknowledges his fraught position within the context of the foster care system. "I got an A in my earth science project, an A on my midterm paper in English, a B-plus in math, and an A in art" (79) he reflects, returning to the mental calculations about his value that do not add up with his reality. He continues:

> If I wasn't so old, Brother Samuel told me, I would be a prime candidate for adoption, so old and so big, you scare them, they want little boys. If they'll take black kids, they want mulattoes and girls. Whatever they want, they don't want black boys. I guess my question, even though I'm only thirteen, is what kind of motherfucker is Brother Samuel to sit up and tell me some shit like that? I don't know if I want to be adopted anyway. What would I do in a family now? Next month, January, I'll be fourteen. (79)

In his reaction, he reveals a sense of self still intact. Aware enough to recognize some malice or manipulation in Brother Samuel's words, Abdul thinks critically about the lack of boundaries and the attempts to instill hopelessness into a youth. In this way, he is able to remove himself, revealing an ego that is healthy enough to observe and question. His reflection bespeaks an awareness of himself subjected to a general category that does not respect his individual strengths. However, this recognition of adult betrayal costs him profoundly, and he understands his increasing devaluation within this system.

Within this Catholic institution, not only does Abdul receive a message about the impossibility of his securing a stable future place within a family, but his identity and family connections are also denied. He discovers eventually that the Brothers knew about his living relatives, but they chose to ignore this information because they "liked him" (88). In one of the saddest moments, Sapphire forces the reader to consider Abdul's alternative. We already know from Precious's story what his life might have been like if he had been raised by Mary Jones. These were his choices: to be raised in complete poverty by a violent, emotionally abuse sexual predator or in a structured environment, with a potential for education, with violent, emotionally abusive sexual predators.

Not only had the Brothers knowingly held him as at St. Aethenlis, but his identity was erased by someone who had used his mother's records to commit public assistance fraud. The social worker tries to explain to Abdul:

> And she didn't want to be—couldn't be—bothered with face-to-face appointments, home visits, and all that, and this woman had to have access to or was in the social service system. She actually got possession of your mother's death certificate—don't ask me how—copied it, and altered it to say a . . . a little boy, you, had died. This false certificate was actually filed with us, and you went on record as dead. (158–59)

Rather than bring the criminal to justice, the system covers up the evidence to avoid a scandal. "And the water comes behind you and washes the footprints away? Most of what I've told you is being washed away as we speak," the investigating social worker explains (160). Abdul replies, "So I just got fucked" (163). He again witnesses himself as an object within a system that does not care about any real damage done to his life. There will be no investigation. The evidence will be washed away. Abdul must confront repeatedly the fact that he cannot rely on recognition or validation from external, societal sources. Later, he ages out of foster care and requires some form of identification to gain employment. He has no identity papers, nothing to prove who he is. His identity has been in the hands of a system that kept careless records and that covered up any errors or evidence of wrongdoing. The perpetrators and bystanders will always attempt to erase the evidence, he learns. For Abdul, there will be no tribunal, truth commission, or reparations.

In *The Kid*, this erasure seems closely connected to the violence that surrounds Abdul. In some ways, the violence Abdul commits serves as radical gestures of control and against erasure, particularly when he acts out in his circumstances. He often retreats into fantasies of himself as a Native American warrior or a king who fells his enemies, imaginary gestures that create a figure of agency. Indeed, his body has been programmed to understand violence as a form of agency, and through the abusive conditioning at the hands of the Brothers, his body associates sexuality—a primal source of creativity—with destruction and pain.

Critics of *The Kid* often object to Sapphire's relentless portrayal of violence and sexual abuse as a kind of "misery porn." For example, Joan Smith's "Misery by the Bucketload" review in London's *Sunday Times* asserts scathingly: "The follow-up to the novel that became the hit film Precious is so consistently grim you almost want to laugh." In these reactions, there is the sense that Sapphire exaggerates and exploits or sensationalizes to sell books and draw media attention. The accusations are not direct, but they exist nonetheless and serve as a reminder of the deep denial that exists on a cultural level when confronting sexual, emotional, and physical exploitation of boys, particularly male children of color. Scholars will need to question this immediate critical response and examine carefully the ways in which Sapphire tests our capacity for compassion and our propensity for stereotyping/demonizing, instead of considering potential culpability in relation to the rape culture in which he grows up. We must remind ourselves constantly that he is a child. In an interview with *SF Weekly*, Sapphire responds to these objections: "In *The Kid*, there is not a gratuitous use of graphic and raw content but a calculated exposure of this kind of content for the express purpose of allowing a reader to see into the soul and circumstances of the characters I create"

(Interview). Abdul's story challenges us in several ways, particularly in the inescapable nature of the violence against his young body at the hands of multiple perpetrators. It is a challenge to identify with a character so incessantly and graphically abused. The reader may need some respite, but since there is very little for the character, there is very little for the reader. In addition, Abdul responds often with rage and aggression to the severe mistreatment. Readers drawn to his mother's portrayal may not find anyone recognizable here. Abdul's responses test our limits when it comes to children as perpetrators of violence. We want to maintain a sense of children as incapable of real aggression and predation. If they do commit terrible acts, they become marked as "bad seeds," or "damaged" beyond repair. Unlike *Push*, *The Kid* critiques "good victim" paradigms that allow us to feel a sense of sympathy and distance within clear boundaries.

From the moment he begins his new life, Abdul encounters unspeakable acts of violence at the hands of Batty Boy, a thirteen-year-old foster child. His next placement in a Catholic boys' home evokes the recent scandals in the Catholic Church, and the portrayal of St. Aethenlis echoes Ireland's Commission to Inquire into Child Abuse and other more recent exposure of the pervasive, endemic sexual, emotional, and physical abuse within Catholic children's homes. As a culture, we are only recently coming to terms with the sexual and emotional exploitation of boys through the controversial reports about the elite Horace Mann and Brooklyn Poly Prep school involving male students. The Sandusky case rocked Penn State and college athletics, with particular attention paid to the victims' vulnerability based on race. These institutions of boyhood or supposed safe havens where masculine youth can develop have been exposed as prime territory for predators. The *Chicago Defender*'s Danny Bakewell asks, "While state and federal law prohibit the identity of a sexual crime victim from being released (no matter what age) it is interesting that no one is discussing the race of these young victims. Which also leads one to ask if these boys would have been young white males would the code of silence and veil of secrecy remained so strong and so quiet for so long?" In a *Philadelphia Tribune* piece, Daryl Gale considers the issues raised if Sandusky "admitted to a simple matter of believing that the innocence of a Black child is less important than that of a white one. Especially if your way of thinking is that these kids are damaged anyway—so one more indignity won't matter much. That too would provide some insight into the twisted mind of a monster, and may even explain some of his actions." Gale raises these issues but allows that the public will likely never have an admission or direct connection validated by the perpetrator.

According to Shirley Jülich, abused children become vulnerable to Stockholm Syndrome, which involves an identification with some aspect of the perpetrator, when they fulfill certain conditions marked by captivity. Jülich finds that unlike victimized adults, "who might retain pre-existing undamaged sense of self, children are in the process of developing their sense of self. Survivors of child sexual abuse appeared to have difficulty in separating psychologically from the offender" (127). For Abdul, this identification manifests itself with his somnambulant predatory behavior, which also serves as an attempt to have emotional and development needs met through sexual abuse, his only association with physical contact. His abusers also train his body to betray Abdul and condition him to associate pleasure and brutality, a form of identification with the perpetrator and against an exploited self. In one devastating but likely routine moment, Brother Samuel rapes Abdul and then clips his navel to keep him silent. Abdul's body responds and tries to feel pleasure from the only intimacy he receives as a child. Then the pleasure is immediately connected to pain. Later, Abdul reflects, "It was just our world, what else were we gonna do? The brothers had us, me, I figured; I thought he, the kids, loved me. I thought that was love" (315). Sapphire brings us to the painful moment when an abuse victim experiences sexual pleasure, when the body responds automatically, which reminds readers of the painful moment in *Push* when Precious turns against herself after she experiences orgasm under the abuse. In *The Kid*, the perpetrator seals a connection between the pleasure response and excruciating physical pain for the victim and shapes identification with the perpetrator as a powerful puppet-master over one's basic bodily responses, although the violence itself is not aestheticized in its representation. It is clearly ugly and the perspectives of the perpetrators clearly distorted. The audience is never drawn into identifying with the violence itself. There is almost strategic use of blackouts and dissociation, although many other moments are almost unbearably graphic. It is more relentless in making us witness the complexity of Abdul's experience. Brutality in part comes from this child whose mother raised him to expect a great deal from the world and who never wavered in his understanding that he was smart. What makes him difficult perhaps for many reviewers to deal with is that his ego is intact as he experiences various assaults/violations. He is angry and questions.

It becomes clear that Abdul-as-predator operates within a trauma schema that includes severe dissociation. His relationship to his developmental need for affection and connection has been corrupted by the extreme abuse. When he abuses a younger boy, Abdul remains in a dreamlike state accompanied by sensory recollections of his own assault by Brother Samuel:

> I can't hear it no place but in my head. It just bangs in my head CLAK CLAK CLAK CLAK fucking with me and fucking with me CLAK CLAK. Big bear-ass motherfucker pressing down, balls in my face, hair red wires in my mouth, the quiet loud like in science-class flicks where time-lapse photography amplifies sounds you don't usually hear like silk being ejected from the spinnerets in the spider's belly. The floor is sticky, I pad past Malik, Omar, Angel, Richard, Bobby, Amir, Jaime. Behind me the aisle is burning. I'm moving like in a dream now. Maybe I am in my dreams. Maybe this is not

real. It is a dream. I dream I'm walking toward the exit sign, I push the door open and walk out into the hall. (71)

In relation to the assaults, Abdul imagines himself more powerful and denies any accountability: "I get up, fly down the aisle. I didn't hurt nobody, do nothing bad. I'm not bad. I'm a good king. I think about flying out the window over my bed, but it's too high up. The light breaks in through cracks in the curtains and slashes me" (64). These difficult moments disturb also because they are romanticized or poeticized in Sapphire's attempt to represent an artistic personality—even as an adolescent sexual offender. We see the way that an aesthetic or creative sensibility merges with deep desire and deprivation in a young psyche. The fantasy and dissociation merged together reveal the constant tension between erasure and assertions of autonomy that mark Abdul's experience as a survivor and artist.

Sapphire also complicates Abdul's identification with the Brothers' predation with the contrast between the acts of violence he commits in this dissociative state and the extremely violent yet clearly controlled fantasies he has about the Brothers once he leaves the home (167–68). The violence spirit may be off-putting to the reviewers and readers. However, these extreme thoughts do not reveal a propensity for violence. Judith Herman explains, "Feelings of rage and murderous revenge fantasies are normal responses to abusive treatment. Like abused adults, abused children are often rageful and sometimes aggressive" (104). He has these fantasies once he leaves the Brothers' home. However, while he is there and completely within their control, his actions must be viewed as a reflection of his vulnerability since "In situations of captivity, perpetrator becomes the most powerful person in the life of the victim, and the psychology of the victim is shaped by the actions and beliefs of the perpetrator" (Herman 75). Given his upbringing and the culture surrounding him, how can we not see his actions as desperate attempts at self-preservation? Predation here conflates with a will to live and exercise some control in the only way he has witnessed and not to succumb to an existence as raw matter acted upon. As readers, we loved Precious because she did not victimize anyone and found more generative ways to express her abjectness. Precious's salvation came in the form of Abdul. Abdul's survival strategies may be uglier and less socially acceptable. They also involve a more isolated journey toward self through art and perhaps highlight a male survivor's isolation and invisibility. Our rejection of Abdul's predation results from a rigid orthodoxy around the victim/perpetrator dynamic, particularly when it comes to sexual predation.

Later, Abdul acts out with violence more consciously and directly when he beats up a white john who attempts to lure him into recording sexual acts and shows him child pornography created with African American male children. While expressing righteous outrage, Abdul's conscience intervenes, "I look around the room for something to smash him in the head with, although a little voice in me is saying stop, enough already" (341). This anger at the source of an immediate threat represents an improvement in his inner work toward resiliency than his earlier claim: "I got no fight in me, flight either. Fight or flight, instinctual mechanism for survival in animals. I'm thirteen I feel like I'm ninety" (74). In these desperate circumstances, violence becomes an assertion of a life force against the spiritual death that threatens to overtake him and his sense of utter disconnect from any sense of agency. Although the acts perpetrated against others shock, the most frequent manifestation of this survival impulse involves violence against the self.

Self-harm is a classic part of survivor syndromes, and "abused children discover at some point that the feeling of [overwhelming fear] can be effectively terminated by a major jolt to the body . . . through the deliberate infliction of [self-]injury" (Herman 109). In *The Kid*, Abdul manages extreme anxiety by trying to control the kind of damage done to his body. When he knows that he will face Brother Samuel's abuse later in the day, for example, he feels compelled to seek a solution to the agony of waiting by hurting himself at the table: "I pick up my fork and jam it HARD into my left hand. The blood seeps out like steam out a valve. I feel relieved. Look up and Brother Samuel is standing over me" (74). Later, when faced with the rejection from the home he has known for five years and the displacement occurring when he finds himself with a great-grandmother he did not know he had, he stifles the emotional turmoil by smashing his head into a mirror. His response to the pain of the cuts is to get an erection. His sexuality is so enmeshed with terror and physical pain, it is an automatic response.

In addition to the physical acts against the self, Abdul also joins his oppressors in wanting to obliterate any evidence of his origins. When Abdul meets his great-grandmother Toosie and leaves the boy's home, we see him begin to gain access to the truth of his history. However, this new access to his family's past repulses him and feels like another violation: "A roach is crawling out a big crack in the linoleum toward me, ain't even afraid. I don't get this, I got a home, a bed. I feel like someone cut my heart out and is eating it in front of me. I feel stupid, wild, lonely, like after my mother die everything just fall apart" (92). Collective memory and family history is not privileged here. His family memory is ugly and painful in the scene of forced witness between Abdul and Toosie. He does not want the information or truth about her personal history. The less he knows, the more he is able to distance himself from her as a possible outcome.

As an orphan who has had his identity threatened on multiple fronts, Abdul's journey toward a viable self involves family history. However, this family history reinforces a sense of the inescapabilty of abjectness and violence, and Abdul finds himself rejecting any connection to his past. Perhaps most painful for readers of *Push* is his impulse to repress his connection to Precious. There may come a time in his life when he can remember Precious safely, but for now, the pain of mother-loss conjures all traumatic experiences that follow: "Remember my mom? What for? It hurts to remember a home, somebody who loved you, maybe it would be better if it was always shit. 'Cause this shit here makes me want to kill something, Mommy's little boy going to be something one day" (155). Abdul even rejects the journals Precious kept to document her rise to literacy: "These notebooks are some kind of indictment or . . . or judgment. They're not normal" (232). When he scatters the notebooks, obliterating the record of his mother's journey to self, he mimics the erasure he has faced at the hands of his abusers and the social service system.

In this instance, however, the desire to destroy all connection to the past may involve a more generative than destructive impulse. Julin Everett asserts that this complicated relationship to the past often characterizes postcolonial orphan autobiographies:

> Like many implicitly retrospective life-narratives, the orphan's autobiography may attempt to resurrect the imagined ancestors of the abandoned child. However, the fissure between the orphan and his or her origins renders the author's account of history incomplete or inaccurate. The success of the autobiographical orphan narrative is thus not only in its engagement in the archeology of one's origins, but also in its emphasis on the creation of a personal history. It is a bildungsroman in the truest sense; a genesis which requires the will of the author to become his or her own creator. (46)

In spite of his agitated resistance, Abdul receives something of value from bearing witness to his family history in his final moments with his only living relative. Toosie's personal story broadens Abdul's understanding of intergenerational violence and sexual exploitation:

> It's like a movie only it ain't. I close my eyes, pictures, the pictures is screaming. All around me blood, Beymour, the brothers, Richie

Jackson. Fifty years. I start crying. Rocking. Sorry. So sorry. I get up off the bed. I feel so sorry love her so much. She's noddin', someplace else, her story over. Water is rolling down my face. I take the kaleidoscope out of the suitcase and lay it at her feet. Bye, Toosie. Bye, Great-Gran'ma. I close the suitcase. Where? I don't know—I don't want to live like her, I don't want to be like her—I do know I'm outta here. (205–6)

He needs to leave 805 and break from his family, yet in one sharp moment, he connects with love to his grandmother's traumatic history. Abdul has heard her story and calls her by her relational name, but then he will not do as she wishes—for him to stay in that space of death and decay and keep the "rent-controlled" apartment. He takes a risk and leaves for his own self-preservation.

This rejection of origins comes with a heavy price and does not provide complete release: "I'm tired of hiding," Abdul asserts, "Well, I'm not hiding, but what is it if nobody knows your name, where you live, who you live with? Everything's been made up, my age, name, what else is there?" (230). In *Push*, we see the betrayal occurring at the hands of the people closest—mother and father. In *The Kid*, the traditional family is obliterated. The child's vulnerability is defined by the absence of a connection to biological origins. What replaces these origins is exploitation within culturally constructed institutions. To survive, Abdul taps into his imagination and rewrites the script: "Delete that shit! I ain't there no more: My mother died in a car accident, and my father got killed in the war. After that, I went to live with my grandmother. Then I got a job and started to live by myself. I'm a normal person I'm a normal person I'm a normal person just like everybody else just like everybody else just like everybody else" (211). Even in the psychiatric hospital at the novel's end, when Abdul must narrate a personal past and assert an identity that will allow his release, he continues to rely to his ability to create a new self. The doctor requires Abdul to acknowledge his history and to recount the events that led him there. Until he has narrated the past, he cannot leave the involuntary confinement. However, it becomes clear that this gesture of remembering does not return him to Toosie, Mary, his father, or even directly to Precious. Instead, he begins to see that he may have had violent impulses and committed predatory acts under certain conditions but that these manifestations of his abuse do not define him. Instead, he activates a new relationship to self through dance, one through which he can rewire the connections between body, agency, and identity.

When reflecting on the relationship between memory and dance, Bill T. Jones claims,

> Even those of us who have no notion of what the auction block was can still feel it, as if the memory is handed down to us through our mother's milk... It is there with me when I dance... My eroticism, my sensuality is often coupled with wild anger and belligerence... I am a person with history-and that history is in part the history of exploitation. (qtd. in Jackson 228)

The Kid forces us to consider abuse and the posttraumatic experience from the perspective of a gifted child, one who may perpetuate the erasure of his family history in conscious, narrative form, but who also engages in Bill T. Jones's self-actualizing memory dance. As a child narrator, Abdul is more sophisticated than one would anticipate given the circumstances of his birth and early years. However, as we get glimpses of his childhood with Precious, we see that he was exposed to cultural resources and encouraged to ask questions. Even in some of his most violent moments, we see this spirit and imagination, and Abdul places his desire for dance in relation to his struggle with the constant threats to his identity: "I try to figure out how and what it is, where or how I fit in, can't—just know this is where I want to be and where I am, and I don't really give a fuck about anything else" (77). Sapphire describes the relationship between traumatic memory and dance in Abdul's experience:

> One of the things I wanted to do was show how pain breaks the connection one has to one's own body and by extension the connection one has to the world. But I also wanted to show how that connection can be rebuilt, re-established, and nurtured. I did not think basketball, geology, or even painting or photography (for a minute I had thought of Abdul having a camera or notebook and "recording" his environment and through that means understanding his life). These things might have been interesting but would they have restored the site—the child body, the black male body his body—that had been the recipient of so much pain? While these other disciplines probably weren't going to do that for him, dance did. (Interview)

He wants nothing more than to remove himself from painful history and the connection to dance. In *The Kid*, dance returns the self to a sense of mastery over the body's place in time and space.

Dance suspends Abdul an eternal present from which he has no desire to escape. Roman, the celebrated dance teacher with whom Abdul trades sex for a home after he leaves Toosie, asserts: "For now that is your turnout! You wish for more, you work for more, but right now that is what you got, and dancers we live in now" (162). This declaration resonates with Abdul's clarity when he dances, and he finds himself feeling utterly alive in dance: "I listen to the beat, bah dah dah DAH! One two three FOUR! I don't care what it's about, I just wanna do it! I start to move across the floor, the drums seem like my own heart beating" (113). The ebb-and-flow of life force becomes quickly and irrevocable entwined with dance: "Before I hear the last drumbeat, I know it's gonna happen—that when I hear the last drumbeat, I'm gonna collapse. That all of a sudden my body will feel like it's been arrested, jumped on, arm twisted, run all over Harlem twice, chemical sprayed, sewed up, and drugged up—that when the music stops, the room will go round and round and I'll fall like broken glass" (114). At fourteen, he acknowledges his intense fragility. He asserts repeatedly his ability to feel alive and connected to his present and creative resiliency through bodily mastery: "My sweat, can the girl next to me smell it? It's not like I feel happy, it's that I don't feel dead when I'm here. I feel I got to do something but I don't know what so I'm doing this" (136). Abdul can manage memory while he's dancing; the fear and sense of impending obliteration leave his body: "It's that way when I get to moving like a gate opens and buffalo stampede, everything comes rushing out of me at once. It's like I remember everything that ever happened to everyone" (140). Dance is liberation, a claim he makes on his own identity through his body: "The opposite of grace is disgrace, dirt, polices, lies, sperms. I want it off my body. Off my body, my body of a free boy, felt good to shit. My body of dance, felt good to dance. Fuck them! Fuck all that shit 'cept dance" (119).

He begins his journey back into being through African dance, which provides a connection to a larger cultural framework that collective, familial, and personal trauma has disrupted for Abdul. Nicole Monteiro and Diana Wall describe the relationship between healing and dance that *The Kid* also advances:

> In many societies, rituals incorporating dance can make use of its ability to serve as a healthy psychological defense mechanism, which allows psychologically or socially unacceptable impulses to be expressed and worked through in sublimated forms. Dance forms, permit individuals to experience chaos symbolically and without danger. Emotions such as anxiety, fear, love and aggression may be incorporated in song and dance, and symbolized through dance and other cultural traditions. (239)

Abdul's response to his first exposure to African dance reinforces this complexity of emotions worked through and within the experience: "Another guy picks up a flute and starts to blow. It's so beautiful it hurts, feels like someone just kicked me in the balls! Then wild, man! Wild! Maybe it's the Black Thai. Maybe, but it's still real. Something stops screaming in my head" (67). As he dances, Abdul reflects about his relationship to his body and claims its wholeness and visibility:

> The way my black tights are holes and raggedy like Jesus in a way makes my thighs look more perfect. I look in the mirror on the opposite wall, which reflects the mirror on this wall and is endlessly repeating my body! The mirror is magic! Giving yourself back to you over and over again. We step away from the barre to center floor in front of Roman, who is standing in front of the mirror. (182)

His body's reflection creates its legacy in the repetition of images, a legacy that he can trace at will in controlled gestures both before and behind him. Here we see again that *The Kid* does not privilege the "recovery narrative" that involves recovering lost narratives from the grips of traumatic evacuation of meaning because understands the complex politics around invisibility and distortion of survivor testimony, particularly for marginalized individuals. Although Abdul faces an inability to locate himself within a suitable narrative or a clear relationship to his past, he discovers dancing as a figuring-forth into selfhood, which stands in contrast with the violation, rejection, and constant threats of erasure.

The origins Abdul feels drawn to involve this sense of creative mastery and begins to claim a connection to a legacy. He has regained his sense of wonder when he considers art, such as when he reads Greg Tate's essay in *Flyboy in the Buttermilk* on Basquiat:

> Why is it significant to me? Okay, some of his intellectual obsessions: ancestry and modernity, originality and the origins of knowledge, personhood and property, possession (in the religious

sense), slavery. . . . Why is it significant to me? I don't know; I don't have words like that inside me; when I think, it's with a contraction of my torso, or a leap like a fucking savage. Savage! OOga BOOga. I'm gonna be like those paintings, like everything I ever loved. I'm gonna be that. And that means off your ass and PRACTICE till you drop. (251)

For Abdul, his ability to manage language through his body surpasses a desire to struggle with words and to attempt to manage meaning beyond expressions made in the present with the "contraction of [a] torso." He answers text with gesture, responding to *Push*'s investment in intertextual healing through Langston Hughes, Alice Walker, among other African American literary figures, with something more urgent, immediate, and transient to reflect Abdul's experience.

In representing this boy, interrupted, at its core, *The Kid* rejects any formulas for complete recovery and relief. Even after we witness Abdul find his life in dance, we must acknowledge that he remains profoundly vulnerable. In the final section, Abdul has a flashback at the opening of the performance in which he has a feature role and self-harms, leading to his institutionalization. At the hospital, his identity is confused with a suspected terrorist: "After that," his doctor tells him, "the police, who had posted an APB for a young man thirty years old, Abdul-Azi Ali—" "That's not my name!" "You didn't know your name—" "That's no reason to do what you did!" "It may not be the reason, but it's part of why. The obvious reason is, we could. You need to not forget that." (367). During his hospitalization, he undergoes electric shock therapy, which again erases his memory, and he also faces violent treatment at the hands of guards who criminalize his confused behavior. Something critical happens in this association between a Black youth whose enters a hospital for attempted suicide and who is then marked as a threat to national security. It is a bit of an imaginary stretch, but it also speaks of a time of profiling and heightened, nebulous anxiety about threats in black hoodies and the ways in which this projected anxiety interferes with young lives.

In *Wrong Place, Wrong Time: Trauma and Violence in the Lives of Young Black Men,* John A. Rich reflects on his experience as a researcher and clinician with the stereotypes that can hinder the ability to understand the traumatic impact of violence:

> I expected that along the way I would meet at least a few young sociopaths whose stated purpose in life was to wound and injure others. In truth, I have met few of these, if any. Yet as I moved from hospital to agency to community, I heard these young people talked about in ways that were more animal than human. Phrases like "endangered species" are easily applied to young black men without considering the unfortunate implication that they are a different "species." (197)

In Abdul's encounter with a compassionate clinician who attempts to see beyond the erasure of individual identity that led him to his current hospitalization, he is asked whether he has ever forgiven anyone. Abdul answers "no" (354). In part, we see through Abdul's experience that forgiveness requires a sense of accountability, memory, and history ... and identity. Abdul's identity has shifted and been erased or rearranged so many times, it remains impossible for him to move toward forgiveness at that moment. Unlike Precious, who finds a community in which she can begin to share trauma's burden of isolation, Abdul remains alone, a strong individual and artist within himself, facing constant threats to his bodily and psychic integrity. The responsibility rests with the readers to affirm their commitment to him and to challenge any self-protective impulse to render him a member of an "endangered species." When the door at the novel's end opens, and Abdul is urged to go, we must continue to move with him, hope he finds the dance in this perpetual escape, and echo his words, "I hear."

CHAPTER 5

"YOU'RE YOUNG, YOU'RE BLACK, AND YOU'RE ON TRIAL. WHAT ELSE DO THEY NEED TO KNOW?"

Reading Walter Dean Myers's *Monster*

That is why I take the films of myself. I want to know who I am.... I want to look at myself a thousand times to look for the one true image.
—Steve Harmon, sixteen-year-old protagonist, *Monster*

In Walter Dean Myers's 1999 young adult novel *Monster*, we meet sixteen-year-old Steve Harmon, an aspiring filmmaker who is on trial for murder. The story unfolds in distinct forms—Steve's prison journal, the courtroom scenes, and significantly, his scripting for a film he plans as he awaits his fate. Through each format, Steve attempts to revise his role within the racialized moral panic that denies due process to Black male teens. Steve's carefully crafted representation of his experience stands in contrast with pervasive cultural narratives that mark him as a presumptive threat and therefore place him at-risk for state-sanctioned or vigilante violence. While cultivating this self-awareness and bearing witness to himself as a Black adolescent male caught within the judicial system, he revises the scripts of other young men of color, such as Jordan Davis, Trayvon Martin, George Stinney, Michael Brown, and the Exonerated Five, who, in the incidents leading to their premature deaths, in the press, and during the connected trials, suffered a paradoxical invisibility while overexposed. Steve both scenes and sees himself within the framework that amplifies stereotypes regarding his Blackness, his youth, and his maleness and frees himself by documenting his personal revelations about the forces that attempt to bind him.

This book began with a chapter focusing on a play set in the late 1960s, a period of transition from the civil rights era. A thread that connects these framing chapters involves the mainstream media's representation of Black youth as antisocial with a propensity for violence without cause and presumed guilt. In "Documenting Social Issues: Black Journal, 1968–1970," Tommy Lee Lott points out a connection between the representation and uprisings of that early point in the post–civil rights era: "In its report on the 1967 urban riots the Kerner Commission cited the coverage of Black community issues by white-oriented mass media as a factor that influenced rebellions" (71). The "Kerner Commission mandate" indicated the need for changes in representations of African Americans by white-oriented mass media, including more nuanced depictions of complex issues underlying any destruction, a more balanced representation that did not only entail alleged criminal activity, and an intentional movement away from presumptions of guilt. However, this recommendation went largely unheeded in mainstream media and political rhetoric in the thirty plus years between the Kerner Report and *Monster*'s 1999 publication.

Three years before *Monster*, then first lady Hillary Clinton made her now infamous comments about a generation of "super predators" while speaking publicly in support of the Crime Bill (Boghani). The controversy did not attempt to minimize the painful aftermath caused by violent crime; rather, objections addressed the way the racialized term dehumanized young people and marked them as irredeemable and that as a society, we must "bring them to heel" as an immediate response. It is well known that Clinton's use of animalistic language in relation to the young people and societal response haunted her during the 2016 election. The controversy sparked a re-engagement with then Princeton professor John J. DiIulio Jr.'s scholarship that gave academic credence to the idea that "America is now home to thickening ranks of juvenile 'super-predators'—radically impulsive, brutally remorseless youngsters, including ever more preteenage boys, who murder, assault, rape, rob, burglarize, deal deadly drugs, join gun-toting gangs and create serious communal disorders" (Bennett et al. 27). This research corresponds to the age of mass incarceration as documented notably by Marc Mauer's *The Race to Incarcerate* and Michelle Alexander's *The New Jim Crow*. In *From #BlackLivesMatter to Black Liberation*, Keeanga-Yamahtta Taylor: "They went farther than resuscitating the "culture of poverty" narrative, reaching back to earlier theories of biological racism. For example, one conservative described urban slums as "human cesspools . . . into which our worst human problems have flowed and in which, through some kind of bacterial action" (50). Taylor notes one conservative author's describing urban rebellions as little more than "outbreaks of animal spirits and of stealing by slum dwellers" (51). These characterizations exemplify the dehumanization, which markedly included youth of color.

The 1989 case of the Central Park Five, now referred to as the Exonerated Five, perhaps most notably demonstrates the ensuing moral panic of the post–civil rights era in relation to Black urban youth and crime. Journalist Natasha Byfield identifies the case's significance as she describes her experience reporting on the arrest of Black and brown teenagers, whose ages ranged from fourteen through sixteen years old, for the brutal rape of a white female jogger: "It reshaped the margins of race, class, and gender for black and brown low-income males for years to come. The coverage likely contributed to changes in the way we address juvenile justice, with profound consequences for the life outcomes of juveniles of color. Thus, the case stands as a uniquely important element in the evolution of our race-based social structure" (4). Similar to

Clinton's later objectifying "super-predator" characterization, the term "wilding" became central to the mythic proportions necessary for moral panic, including ascribing superhuman strength while eradicating any humanity, and "looking carefully at the linguistic structure of the term wilding, it is difficult to overlook its wild essence; one can intuitively interpret wilding as a threat conceived as menacing, savage, untamed, uncivilized, erratic, unruly, and ferocious" (Welch 14).

When commenting on the reception of the Ken Burns *Central Park Five* documentary, Patricia Williams addresses the role of racial identity in documentary filmmaking and the ways in which Black filmmakers and critics authority to tell the stories of Black communities in relation to justice issues are questioned:

> I wonder if this film would be having the same reception had a black filmmaker made it. Would a Charles Burnett or John Singleton have had to negotiate suspicion about motives and sympathies that white directors, positioned in not a few minds as inherently neutral and unbiased, do not? That's a terrible thought all by itself: if in 2013 we remain as quietly committed to the same counterfactual presumptions of veracity, guilt and "reality" that we did in 1990, then this film documents only a terrible history repeating itself over and over again.

Williams raises important questions about the role of the filmmaker's race in the reception of documentaries that present counternarratives and question our society's foundational institutions. Although Black filmmakers may face unjust concerns about bias when treating controversial issues, such as those raised in the Central Park Five film, the documentary or docudrama genre provides a vehicle to resist stereotypes and present a more nuanced reality.

Monster's documentary-making becomes transparent, and the story told unfolds with the novel's plot as the artist and subject merge. Considering the potential for "absence and distortion" of his story, Steve Harmon engages in a "political act" as he "reinvents" himself through the agency of artistic process. Before he found himself at the center of his own film, Steve's life revolved around his family, his neighborhood, and his studies at Stuyvesant, one of the most academically rigorous public high schools in the United States with a 100 percent college-bound rate. Steve has achieved clear recognition as an academically gifted teen and is therefore already vulnerable to the challenges of giftedness that Johnnas faced. He decides to use his school experience with scene blocking to document his experience and begins to write a script to a film called *Monster*, based on the prosecutor's name for him, which raises immediately the question, What would it mean to be placed in this environment abruptly and to have the label of "monster"? Engaging on multiple levels with themes of alienation and estrangement, as much as Steve's documentary is an artistic piece that comments critically on the justice system in relation to Black youth, it is also an art documentary, focusing on the creative development of the young Black person. The courtroom scenes include specific testimony that names Steve as a young artist publicly. He has a mentor, Mr. Sawicki, who identifies him as an insightful and promising young filmmaker and who speaks about the aesthetic values Steve brings to his work. What does it mean for a young filmmaker who wishes to document his reality and community that he will find himself "in the wrong place at the wrong time"? What opportunities does he have outside of taking this risk to remain true and authentic to his craft?

Steve finds himself on trial after several codefendants identify him as an accomplice in a robbery that resulted in a shop owner's murder. As an artist, Steve does not seek to distance himself from either his community, local environment, or himself as a young Black man caught up in the criminal justice system. In Steve's case, he did not pull the trigger but is accused of serving as a lookout who gave a signal to the co-defendants, who entered a local bodega and killed the owner in a robbery attempt. The evidence against Steve is witness testimony, sometimes second hand, and all provided in exchange for plea deals and reduced time. That his alleged crime involves assessing a scene visually seems like a curious coincidence for a young filmmaker who spends his days scouting for possible settings. He observes constantly.

In the opening statements to his trial, we witness prosecutor Petrocelli present a world of citizens versus monsters. She envelopes all involved into this rigid schema, and there is no sense that the defendants, including Steve, are also citizens who have rights and protections under the law. Petrocelli reinforces the dichotomy, leaving no space for nuance: "Most people in our community are decent, hardworking citizens who pursue their own interests legally and without infringing on the rights of others. But there are also monsters in our communities—people who are willing to steal and to kill, people who disregard the rights of others" (21). Petrocelli aligns herself with the "society," "system of laws," "citizens," "I represent the State of New York," and I am part of that system" (21). This move on the prosecutor's part confirms what Elijah Anderson describes in *Against the Wall: Poor, Young, Black, and Male*: "Strongly identified with violent criminality by skin color alone, the anonymous young Black male in public is often viewed first and foremost with fear and suspicion, his counter-claims to propriety, decency, and law abidingness" (3). As a representative of the state, Petrocelli places herself in a position to define the parameters of civic participation and citizenry itself. She demarcates the boundaries between citizens and "monsters," casting the defendants from the sphere of citizenship, thereby denying them the basic rights to due process and presumed innocence through this characterization. Like "super-predators" and "wilding" beasts, "monsters" exist outside the threshold of potential innocence, mitigating circumstance, or redemption. Society must eradicate "monsters" to preserve order.

While she speaks, Steve imposes the word "Monster" repeatedly on a blank sheet, revealing his fascination with this fraught use.

His defense attorney, Ms. O'Brien, interprets his gesture as one of self-doubt, which in part may be true. Petrocelli's words may be invading his self-perception; however, this gesture of repetition on paper also may signal the stimulation of a creative mind. He has identified and isolated a key concept in this whole business and is captivated. Steve's brainstorming connects the strands of creativity and consciousness around the construction of him as a "monster." While O'Brien sees his writing as reifying and self-implicating, Steve connects to his artistic self in this moment, unhinging the concept of "monster" as a predetermined set of racialized cues that corrupt a process supposedly based on due process. His decision to create a documentary rests largely on this moment when he decides to engage conceptually with "monster" as Petrocelli invokes it.

Public defender O'Brien appears resigned to presenting a case in which the presumption of innocence does not apply, and a young person receives no consideration relative to their age. Part of the "race-ing" of the innocent versus the monster includes the scenes that play out of the public spaces of the courtroom or media in which the evidence is already fixed against Blackness.

There is no room for Black innocence here and no room for envisioning the Black child as a child. In these recent circumstances, we see a reversal of roles in that the child's body is rendered menacing, and a predominantly white popular imagination believes that even when an adult is trained and armed, the child is the threat. This dynamic is revealed in Darren Wilson's description of unarmed Michael Born as "Hulk" or "Demon," positioning himself, an armed police officer with access to a vehicle, as a helpless child: "When I grabbed him the only way I can describe it is I felt like a 5-year-old holding onto Hulk Hogan" (Calamur). In the case of Tamir Rice, the twelve-year-old child murdered by a Cleveland police officer within two seconds on the scene for carrying a toy gun, he was often described as "big for his age," suggesting some indiscernibility of age had contributed to his death.

Steve's project can be understood in comparison to recent social media activism that Nicole Fleetwood refers to as "trouble the field of vision." In the wake of the Michael Brown shooting in Ferguson, Missouri, a Black Twitter and Tumblr campaign emerged that responded to selective circulation of images representing Black youth as "thugs." With the hashtag #iftheygunnedmedown, a social media protest featured Black and brown participants offering two disparate images: one that may be interpreted as "thug-like" behavior and one signaling social acceptability, including graduation and family photos. These images establish the distance between the individual and the type and were in part in response to posts that spread misinformation about Brown, including the infamous incident with Kansas City Police officer Marc Catron, who posted an image of a convicted murder under Brown's name. The campaign recalls the "I am Trayvon Martin" campaign on Tumblr in which people dressed up wearing hoodies, and both interventions acknowledge the highly racialized quality of the visual realm. The young people acknowledge that their experimentations and play with their images with "selfies" can circulate through one's social media "footprint" and become misinterpreted or used falsely as evidence of character traits, removed from any original context of youthful invention.

Steve's documentation of his experience in film counters the media frenzy occurring around cases with African American male youth and exposes the way cameras and recordings work within rhetorical frameworks and relationships with audiences. Steve's public defender, O'Brien, must create an association between presumed innocence and her client, although it should exist a priori:

> As Mr. Harmon's attorney all I ask of you, the jury, is that you look at Steve Harmon now and remember that at this moment the American system of justice demands that you consider him innocent. He is innocent until proven guilty. If you consider him innocent, and by the law you must, if you have not prejudged him,

then I don't believe we have a problem convincing you that what the State will produce will challenge his innocence. (26–27)

In this critical moment, Steve identifies the question about his compromised guarantee of presumed innocence. O'Brien continues; she raises the history of lynching and extrajudicial violations of due process: "But the laws also protect the accused, and that is the wonder and beauty of the American system of justice. We don't drag people out of their beds in the middle of the night and lynch them. We don't torture people. We don't beat them. We apply the laws equally to both sides" (26). However, Steve's lens casts her negligence in not seeing the problems within the justice system that continue to haunt the present moment.

In Myers's novel, Steve feels the weight of history and illuminates this corruption of the Black child's image. The youth become the subject of a media campaign: "As the newspapers howled for arrests of the marauding teens and then-mayor Ed Koch called it 'the crime of the century,' real-estate mogul Donald Trump took out ads calling for the return of the death penalty. Trump wanted 'criminals of every age' involved in the Central Park jogger case 'to be afraid.'" (Feeney and Adams Otis). This lack of regard for the age of the alleged offender will also play a significant role in the "1994 'Omnibus Crime Bill' with its section that allows children as young as thirteen to be tried as adults" (Marable 98) and recalls the George Stinney trial in 1944, when the fourteen-year-old, physically incapable of committing the crimes, faced execution after a trial that lasted less than ten minutes. The youngest person legally executed in US history, his sentence aligned with Southern Carolina's particular pattern for sentencing juveniles to death: "It was a punishment reserved exclusively for black children, and almost exclusively for crimes (allegedly) committed by black children involving white victims" (Johnson, Blume, and Freedman 334–35). The history remains relevant today as Steven Harmon explores in his documentary examination of the state's depiction of him as a "monster" begins with removing any association with his young age:

> This misperception of black children as adults persists today. Black children are eighteen times more likely to be sentenced as adults. The age of juvenile black felony suspects is overestimated, with black felony suspects rated as older than white or Latino suspects. Juvenile black suspects were also deemed more culpable for their actions than white or Latino targets, particularly when those targets were accused of serious crimes. The magnitude of this overestimation is huge: black felony suspects were seen as 4.53 years older than they actually were. The consequence is both striking and consistent with the death sentencing of fourteen-year-olds: black boys-today are misperceived as legal adults at roughly the age thirteen-and-a-half. (Johnson, Blume, and Freedman 355)

Steve's interactions with O'Brien confirm that the prosecution's strategy will only strengthen the confirmation bias built on this historical legacy. She entertains not even the slightest possibility that the jurors will grant Steve his legal right to presumed innocence: "Well, frankly, nothing is happening that speaks to your being innocent. Half of those jurors, no matter what they said when we questioned them when we picked the jury, believed you were guilty the moment they laid eyes on you. You're young, you're Black, and you're on trial. What else do they need to know?" (79). His fate relies rather on "how the jury sees the case" (79), which translates clearly into a battle between the prosecutor who stands between them and a menacing force, rather than a sixteen-year-old boy.

Rather than succumb to this process, Steve responds reflexively by composing scenes in his mind. O'Brien's assumptions about Steve's writing also indicate a failure to recognize Steve's ability to remove himself from the moment and to engage in creative analysis. When he writes this word repeatedly, he suspends its meaning in a kind of creative summoning or incantation:

> I think to get used to this I will have to give up what I think is real and take up something else. I wish I could make sense of it. Maybe I could make my own movie. I could write it out and play it in my head. I could block out the scenes like we did at school. The film will be the story of my life. No, not my life, but of this experience. I'll write it down in the notebook they let me keep. I'll call it what the lady who is the prosecutor called me. Monster. (4–5)

From this point forward, Steve presents a scripted version complete with directions to "FADE IN: INTERIOR," for example. The control over the perspective lies with him and his vision. This moment too marks the Black subject's break from himself in the scene, to see himself in that scene within a racialized schema, although this moment provides insight into a forced fracturing of an integrated self-in-the-world imposed by the racialized gaze. Here, however, Steve is seeing himself and others at an artistic remove as part of the process of generating a new text that allows for critical analysis of the various players and their parts. His film training gave him the tools to bear witness to himself amid this traumatic experience. Importantly, Steve does not escape into fantasy when he chooses documentary realism and employs voice-over to capture this choice: "Ain't no use putting the blanket over your head, man. You can't cut this out; this is reality. This is the real deal" (8). The opening credits presented in the form of Star Wars, a gesture toward linking his project with this popular film phenomenon, placing his story within a larger cultural frame. "The incredible story of how one guy's life was turned around by a few events and how he might spend the rest of his life behind bars. Told as it actually happened!" (9).

Steve's orientation toward filmmaking provides a meaningful language with which to frame his experience and provides an opportunity as he lives through this traumatic period for some creative agency, even as he witnesses his own sense of alienation:

Sometimes I feel like I have walked into the middle of a movie. It is a strange movie with no plot and no beginning. The movie is in black and white and grainy. Sometimes the camera moves in so close that you can't tell what's going on and you just listen to the sounds and guess. I have seen a lot of movies about prisons but never one like this. This is not a movie about bars and locked doors. It is about being alone when you are not really alone and about being scared all the time. (4)

The "movie" focuses on the inner life of the young person. In his initial description, there is no definition, no blurred boundaries. It is a muddled state of being overwhelmed. He identifies the isolation that defines prison life. Steve uses his experience as raw material to engage with the lessons provided by his mentor, Mr. Sawicki, and he provides flashbacks to exchanges with his teacher to illuminate his motivations. Most notably, when the jury enters the courtroom, Steve switches the scene to a classroom. This juxtaposition between these two spaces leads to a more nuanced understanding of juries. Through his memory, Steve connects to an understanding of jurying as a process of evaluation based on criteria and elements, expectations, and innovations. They discuss Steve's initially positive assessment of a class project's ending in the classroom scene, and Sawicki replies: "I didn't say it was bad, but wasn't it predictable? You need to predict without predicting. You know what I mean? When you make a film, you leave an impression on the viewers, who serve as a kind of jury for your film. If you make your film predictable, they'll make up their minds about it before it's over" (19). Steve uses his film class instruction to contest the prescribed version of events that would leave no room for his complexity as a young person when he connects "jury" in artistic reception with the legal system. Predictability here becomes a presumption of guilt and the imposition of stereotypes that work against Steve. This connection between the courtroom determinism and the advice from a creative mentor speaks to Steve's ability to alter scripts "the predictability" within his own artistic endeavors. Steve's chosen art form is film, where narrative and visual elements combine to generate meaning. Steve will need to confront this "predictability" in the way he scripts his film and reflects on the process.

The novel centers around his growing awareness of the way he is othered in the experience and offers his attempt at a critical intervention into this Monster. The scripting demonstrates a self-and-situational awareness that counters dehumanization. This creative form is invested in the visual realm and his scripting raises issues of how he is represented and must create counter-images/scripts against and to reveal this monster-ification. Part of his process is to document his experience as a sixteen-year-old in an adult prison. The consequences and lived experiences of youth held in adult prisons do not often register as significant enough to intervene and disrupt the system in part because they remain seldom heard. Steve's promotional line emphasizes both realism and sensationalism: "The incredible story of how one guy's life turned around by a few events and how he might spend the rest of his life behind bars. Told as it actually happened!" Using dramatic punctuation, he becomes the subject of his own inquiry as "16-year-old Steve Harmon as the Boy on Trial for Murder!" (10).

When considering cases from recent history, Kalief Browder and Korey (Kharey) Wise, both sixteen and in adult prisons for crimes they did not commit, seem clearly relevant. Both teens refused to plead guilty and did not accept opportunities for early release that would have caused them to compromise their stances related to innocence. Reporting from the *New York Times* on the released documents related to the Central Park/Exonerated Five case finds:

> The men consistently maintained their innocence and were sometimes punished for it. In a 1999 psychological evaluation released as part of the trove of documents, a psychologist wrote that one of the men, Kharey Wise, participated in a sex offender program in

prison, but "the program identified him as noncompliant because he denies sexually abusing the victim." A handwritten note from Mr. Wise was published as well: "I Wise would like for you to disregard my name for that program you and I talked about," he wrote. Along with detailed evidence and previously unpublished police reports, the documents also reveal something more human: the parallel life that the boys might have lived if they had not been sent to prison. (Mueller et al.)

Coerced confession or attempts at self-implication factor significantly in the historical record around cases like Steve's, particularly in relation to poor Black and brown youth, and Steve's observations counter the efforts to replace his story with a narrative that fits the pressures of expediency imposed from outside himself. He recounts the raw, intimate details of prison life as a teenager incarcerated with adults. "Most of the voices are clearly Black or Hispanic," he notes (7). An inmate uses the bathroom out in full view. "Ain't no use putting the blanket over your head, man. You can't cut this out; this is reality. This is the real deal" (8). This repeated emphasis on "reality" and "real deal" exposes his naivete . . . also the sense that the audience has a thirst for authenticity. There is also the issue of bearing witness to the experience, so he remains visible through his own testimony.

This desire suggests Jennifer Gonnerman's description of her encounter with Kalief Browder, who shares his stories about abuse from guards and inmates at Rikers, stories captured in essence by the videos of his beatings. Browder makes it clear that the brutal videos should serve as a catalyst for change:

We discussed whether they should be published on *The New Yorker*'s website. I told him that it was his decision. He said to put them online. He was driven by the same motive that led him to talk to me for the first time, a year earlier. He wanted the public to know what he had gone through, so that nobody else would have to endure the same ordeal. His willingness to tell his story publicly—and his ability to recount it with great insight—ultimately helped persuade Mayor Bill de Blasio to try to reform the city's court system and end the sort of excessive delays that kept him in jail for so long. (Gonnerman)

Choosing the role of documentarian of his own journey through the criminal justice system is an act of creative agency that allows him to remain grounded in the present and not to dissociate. It is a form of cognitive behavioral modification and emotional regulation that counters the traumatic experience and its potential to overwhelm him. He may seem at a remove from himself or detached, but in fact he is conscious, aware, and naming the situation and its players as he encounters them.

In Steve's scripting of the criminal justice spaces, including the courtroom and precinct, he represents his struggle with seeing the way other people see him and addresses the way he sees and is seen or "scene-d" in a demonizing script. His desire to document this process of dehumanization echoes filmmaker Ava DuVernay's assertion about the subjects of *When They See Us*: "Not thugs. Not wilding. Not criminals. Not even the Central Park Five. They are Korey, Antron, Raymond, Yusef, Kevin. They are millions of young people of color who are blamed, judged and accused on sight." Several interactions highlight how Steve's humanity is similarly effaced. Although his defense attorney appears committed professionally, she remains distant and cold, perhaps desensitized to her client's personal experience. She speaks in cold, clinical terms about his charges. He is told that his charge is felony murder and that "light" would be life in prison. Her manner is blunt and to the facts. She is not warm or reassuring at all, but her directness may best reveal Steve's reality at this moment: "My job is to make sure the law works for you as well as against you, and to make you a human being in the eyes of the jury" (16). A conversation between stenographer and guard reveals the callousness of treatment.

Steve has not gone through a trial, yet they assume they know the outcome. The stenographer wants the trial to last so she can make extra money. There is no regard for the human being whose life is at stake. He is presumed guilty. The guard replies, "Six days—maybe seven. It's a motion case. They go through the motions; then they lock them up. (Turns and looks off camera toward STEVE.) Ain't that right, bright eyes?" (14). The courtroom's main authority figure appears not to maintain a sense of objectivity: "He is a 60-year-old New York judge and already looks bored with the case" (17). This boredom suggests that the judge believes that he will receive no new narrative, nothing to force him back to a state of presence required for true witness. In the courtroom, Steve also encounters a junior high school class and jurors, none of whom looks directly at him. Through these encounters, Steve observes the way his humanity becomes disconnected through a paradoxical hypervisibility and invisibility. When he reacts in despair, lowering his head to cry, his attorney admonishes him: "If you give up, they'll give up on you. (Then angrily) Get your head up!)" (99). However, she fails to acknowledge that he recognizes the ways in which the courtroom has predetermined his outcome. His agency and ability to "keep his head up" moves into the creative realm to offer his testimony and document the process.

Through his scripting, he documents the excruciating experience of witnessing his value as an individual decline. He recalls the interaction with the police detectives in the 28th Precinct, and there is no indication that he had a lawyer or a parent with him (he was 16, so he could be questioned alone). The two detectives questioning talk between each other about Steve's fate: "KARYL: 'They are saying that you pulled the trigger. King said that the score was over but you turned back and shot Nesbitt. Why did you do that? I can't figure it" (71). "WILLIAMS: 'This guy's only 16. They won't kill him.' KARYL: 'What are you, a pessimist? Hope for the best." (73). To tell the whole story, Steve must also represent the painful changes in his relationship with his family. Steve wants to testify and tells his father: "I'm just going to tell the truth, that I didn't do anything wrong" (111). In response to this statement regarding his innocence, Steve must confront his father's grief: "CU of MR. HARMON. There are tears in his eyes. The pain in his face is very evident as he struggles with his emotions" (111). In many ways, Steve must witness the death of himself as his father's son in his meeting with his father: "Seeing my dad cry like that was just so terrible. What was going on between us, me being his son and him being my dad, is pushed down and something else is moving up in its place. It's like a man looking down to see his son and seeing a monster instead" (115). As an artist, Steve does not soften this devastation as his father recalls the child around whom he built his dreams: "When you were first born, I would lie up in the bed thinking about scenes of your life. You playing football. You going off to college. I used to think of you going to Morehouse and doing the same things I did when I was there.... I never thought of seeing you—you know—seeing you in a place like this. It just never came to me that you'd ever be in any kind of trouble" (112). This scene brings the family dynamic into clear focus and eliminates any doubt about the connection between Steve and his family. Steve is from a "good family," yet he faces the same possible labeling as "thug" or similar racialized criminal stereotype.

Within the context of this telling, filmmaker Steve understands the value in fleshing out his character through this poignant display of family intimacy: "The scene blurs and darkens. There is the sound of STEVE's FATHER sobbing" (113). As a director, he chooses to amplify the sound of the grown man suffering in response to his inability to help his son but allows his father the dignity of the blurring and darkening scene. The note that follows the scene indicates the power of including this moment on a personal level as well: "Notes: I've never seen my father cry before. He wasn't crying like I thought a man would cry. Everything was just pouring out of him and I hate to see his face" (115). This moment suggests both the depth of the crisis and an awakening in terms of masculinity and vulnerability. His father allows himself to be vulnerable in front of his son and to express his fear and his grief that his desire to protect his son from racism has failed within these circumstances. As a parent/father, he is utterly helpless and has lost control to the state.

Steve documents the painful grieving process within families during the incarceration process. It is not confirmed that his father has lost sense of his son, but Steve feels a sense of loss, nevertheless. This moment reveals an irreversible pain, traumatic encounter with death even as he lives. Steve witnesses his own death in his father's grieving face. That is the true cost of this reduction into "monster." The father had dreams for the son that he believes at that point will never come to fruition, but the father failed to acknowledge the possibility that his son remains innocent and trapped in between these parental expectations and hopes for escaping racial bias through respectability and a system that will continue to limit Steve's horizon by presuming guilt, not only in this instance but as a general character flaw, as being a *monster*. The plot that does not avoid predictability is this one. As an artist, Steve is committed to showing something beyond the known and obvious, and that departure or innovation includes exposing painful scenes such as the one with his father and mother: "In a way I think she was mourning me as if I were dead" (158). The text includes the mother holding a photo (158), drawing into focus the ways in which mothers in courtrooms curate these images, choosing which images to hold close to represent their children against the stereotypes.

Often used as symbols in the culture wars, children as characters may "provide a means to make a story understandable and the victims and villains knowable" (Beardsely and Teresa 167); however, this understanding of children's function in collective narrative does not apply when race precludes an association with innocence. The parents in these narratives intervene in this "adultification" and serve to counter-interpellate the assessment back toward youth. To rehumanize the teens in the Exonerated Five case, for example, the *Amsterdam News* commissioned a series of articles from Sharrone Salaam, Yusef's mother and a professor at Parsons School of Design, who wrote of her experience watching her son's trial. This response tapped into myths of childhood innocence, stressing in particular the vulnerability of the teens. The mother-son dynamic that framed Salaam's impassioned set of articles was replicated by the journalists of the *Amsterdam News*. Repeatedly, the youthfulness of the teens was evoked in trial coverage, and female reporters typically made those evocations. In one instance, Tanya Haughton and Lisa Isom wrote of McCray, Salaam, and Santana that "close scrutiny shows that they are quite simply three young men who at times seem to be oblivious to the magnitude of the circumstances that is occurring around them" (qtd. in Beardsley and Teresa 172).

The scene of Steve's arrest exposes the lack of transparency and information for parents and children caught in the system. Steve, a teenager and dependent but treated as an adult, witnesses his mother's helplessness when she does not receive any information from the detectives, even though they take Steve into custody within her home without any warrant: "MRS. HARMON: Why are you handcuffing my son if you want to ask him a few questions? I don't understand" (124). Detective Williams tells her that it is "just routine" and "Don't worry about it," to which she responds: "What do you mean don't worry about it, when you're handcuffing my son? . . . I'm coming with you! You're not just snatching my son off like he's some kind of criminal" (125). She tries to get her coat and accompany her son, but there is no consideration given to her as a mother. Steve has not been formally arrested or charged, and he has not been read his rights. It appears to be "routine" to take him away in handcuffs. To his mother, within her home, they are taking her child away: "MRS. HARMON rushes from the house, looks desperately around, and moves quickly down the street. She gets almost to the corner, then stops, realizing she doesn't know where

STEVE is being taken" (126). At sixteen, however, Steve is no longer considered a child and does not require a parent or guardian to be present, similarly to Yusef Salaam and his questioning when the police mistakenly thought he was sixteen, instead of only fifteen.

Steve represents this scene in which he disappears from his mother's view and site or is "disappeared" by state control. By incorporating this scene in his script, he shows his vulnerability in a moment that does not often enter public consciousness around juvenile justice. As the author and director of his experience, Steve also joins this process of intervention, using a variety of texts and cinematic devices, most notably a journal and interjecting flashbacks into courtroom scenes to provide further context and disrupt the trajectory toward sealing his guilt.

Throughout his experience, Steve keeps a journal, and in many ways, the journal provides a space in which he can locate his youth. The journaling serves as a necessary supplement to the more controlled scripting, with its raw material depicting his inner life and unsettled space, to delineate the artistic endeavor from unfiltered self-exploration. The journal balances the courtroom scenes by allowing us not to remain in the visual mode of processing his experience. The scripting allows him to navigate the fraught terrain of visual representation or cultural scene-ing. Also, an important contrast exists between the activist-intervention involved in the scripting in which he uses the tools he learned in school to counter the dominant racist iconography. Then, the shift to vulnerability and intimacy in the journal employs a powerful literary device to reveal Steve's youthful questioning and struggle against erasure of self. Through his journal, we connect with his emotional experience, and most importantly, the journal testifies to his age. He is a young person, very bright, creative, and insightful, but very young, which we see when he writes, for example that "The best time to cry is at night, when the lights are out and someone is being beaten up and screaming for help" (1). The journals also provide insight into Steve's creative process and its soul-sustaining role in his situation: "I looked over the movie again. I need it more and more. The movie is more real in so many ways than the life I am leading. No, that's not true. I just desperately wish this was only a movie" (159). For Steve, scripting keeps him grounded, even as he struggles with maintaining a sense of reality: "Nothing is real around me except the panic. The panic and the movies that dance through my mind. I keep editing the movies, making the scenes right. Sharpening the dialog" (271). He is exposed to random acts of violence and brutality that do not appear to phase the prison authorities but leave Steve with a sense that he will always be in shock but never be numb.

At one point after the judge decides to break for the day, Steve returns to the detention center, and there is no light and no way to capture the scene visually. Instead, the violence is captured in the sound: "It is night; the lights are out except for dim nightlights placed along the walls. We hear fists methodically punching someone as the camera goes slowly down the corridor, almost seeming to look for the source of the hitting. We see two inmates silhouetted, beating a third. Another inmate is on the lookout" (57). It turns out that the beating, which soon becomes a rape, occurs within Steve's cell: "We see the whites of his eyes, then we see him close his eyes as the sounds of the beating stop and the sounds become those of a sexual attack against the inmate who was beaten" (57). The brutal assault occurs within close range to this high school junior. Steve writes notes about the film, "But if I didn't think of the movie I would go crazy. All they talk about in here is hurting people" (45). The randomness of the violence invokes hypervigilance and panic: "If you look at somebody, they say 'What you looking at me for? I'll mess you up'" (45). He balanced this overwhelming urge to be invisible in the prison and not to engage with a need to flesh out a meaningful presence for survival through his scripting.

He describes feeling detached from immediate surroundings and feeling like he is in a movie, not his life: "It's funny, but when

I'm sitting in the courtroom, I don't feel like I'm involved in the case. It's like the lawyers and the judge and everybody are doing a job that involves me, but I don't have a role" (59). Steve documents his estrangement from a situation that attempts to create a type from a full human, primarily through a racialized visual field: "I think they are bringing out all of these people and letting them look terrible on the stand and sound terrible and then reminding the jury that they don't look any different from me and King" (60). Steve understands that he witnesses his undoing and prefers the imaginary realm he creates through his scripting, where he has some agency in determining his representation: "I like the last scene in the movie, the one between me and Jerry. It makes me seem like a real person" (60). Throughout his experience, he exposes his processing to show the threat of possible internalization of the values and projections he faces: "I want to look like a good person. I want to feel like I'm a good person because I believe I am. But being in here with these guys makes it hard to think about yourself as being different. We look about the same, and even though I am younger than they are, it's hard not to notice that we are all pretty young. I see what Miss O'Brien meant when she said part of her job was to make me look human in the eyes of the jury" (63).

Steve includes the testimony of these witnesses and codefendants from whom he must differentiate himself to preserve his rights as an individual on trial. Among the youngest witnesses is fourteen-year-old Osvaldo Cruz. After O'Brien mentions his upcoming testimony to Steve, a scene break occurs in a flashback to an earlier encounter between the youths. Osvaldo taunts Steve, making fun of his gifted program at Stuyvesant High School by using homophobic slurs, but he is cautioned by another youth because Steve "hangs with some bad dudes" (81). Osvaldo's testimony places Steve in the same category as Bobo Evans and James King. He indicates that he participated in the robbery due to intimidation from the three men, which contrasts the previous scene in which Osvaldo appears to antagonize Steve. As he witnesses himself painted broadly through the testimony, he feels growing desperation to claim his sense of self: "I wanted to open my shirt to see who I really was, who the real Steve Harmon was" (92). Guards and public defenders discuss their lives, and Steve observes and recognizes the gap between his current perspective and theirs about life and freedom.

Steve also employs flashbacks as a scripting device, and the flashbacks stand as an intervention in the recreation of his story and history told by institutions and external perspectives. The testimony from witnesses inside the courtroom is tainted by the plea deals and prosecutorial strategies. After Zinzi testifies that he "struck a deal" in relation to information about the case, Steve scripts a flashback to an earlier moment when children navigated accountability: "FLASHBACK of a 12-year-old STEVE walking in a NEIGHBORHOOD PARK with his friend TONY. Tony gets punched for a rock that Steve threw that hit a young woman walking with her boyfriend. 'TONY: I didn't throw that rock. You threw it. STEVE: I didn't say you threw it. I just said 'Run.' You should've run. TONY: I'll get me an Uzi and blow his brains out" (43). In this moment, Steve provides a glimpse of himself and his peer navigating adolescent masculinity and the random way they make decisions about actions and consequences based on this developmental stage as youths.

Another flashback occurs after Bolden testifies that he received the information about the robbery from Bobo Evans: "CUT TO: EXTERIOR STOOP ON 141ST STREET. There is one small tricycle on the sidewalk. It is missing one wheel. The garbage cans at the curb are overflowing. Three young girls jump rope near the trash" (49). Using descriptions of decay near youthful innocence to set a scene for Steve's early encounter with James King, the "mastermind" behind the robbery. Johnny, one of King's friends, addresses Steve as the group discusses ways to get easy money through small-time robbery: "What you got, youngblood? (51). When Steve replies indefinitely. Johnny inquires about him and his standing:

"Yo—what's your name? Steve. Since when you been down?" (51). The scene returns immediately to the courtroom and continues with the Bolden questioning The scene returns immediately to the courtroom and continues with the Bolden questioning.

When Steve learns about Mr. Nesbitt's death, the scene focuses on his basketball. He is holding it when he begins to listen to the neighborhood women talking. Then we see him without the basketball, and then after he runs away: "Camera pans down the street, past playing kids and stores to a basketball that lies in the gutter" (119). Through his editing, he revisits scenes from his youth and creates a space for himself as a child, even as he watches his youth diminish in the eyes of others. The focus on the way Steve is "seen" includes representing the media's interactions with neighbors after the murder. As a director, Steve chooses the objects of childhood: "There was a baseball game on but it didn't look real. It was guys in uniforms playing games on a deep green field. They were playing baseball as if baseball was important and as if all the world wasn't in jail watching them from a completely different world. The world I came from, where I had my family around me and friends and kids I went to school with and even teachers, looked so far away" (156). Through his directorial choices, he highlights the disparity between his previous life, only months before, and the one in which he now exists as someone rendered an adult almost overnight.

Steve names himself as a child against the circumstances that attempt to erase his youth: "They didn't allow kids in the visiting area, which is funny. It was funny because if I wasn't locked up, I wouldn't be allowed to come into the visiting room" (156). Education scholar Chonika Coleman-King considers:

> I wonder if the presumption of adolescence is deleted or if their adolescence means something different.... I wonder if it means that they are more likely to be deviant during adolescence. If an old black man was wearing a hoodie or a younger boy, would the

presumption of criminality be the same? Urban education scholars like Howard C. Stevenson [see Cassidy and Stevenson] have argued that black males in particular aren't seen as children, but I think when you layer that with the idea that adolescence is generally a time where young people act out, it's magnified for kids of color. (Groenke et al. 36)

His younger brother stands as a marker to anchor Steve against this flood of cognitive dissonance: "Jerry was tiny in the street, standing on the corner. The window was screened and I knew he couldn't see me, but I raised my hand anyway and waved to him. I wanted to tell Jerry that I loved him. I also wanted to tell him that my heart was not greatly rejoicing, and I was not singing praises" (157). Through this expression of love towards his younger brother, he raises his hand to wave at a version of himself, to connect to his humanity through his brother, though he stands minimized in the distance.

Steve's depiction of his experience in the criminal justice system also factors in the political opportunity his situation offers, specifically when referring to Rudy Giuliani's proclamation that he is "determined to stop crime in all areas of the city.... The idea that we're just trying to stop crime in white or middle class areas is nonsense. Everyone living in the city deserves the same protection" (122–23). Henry Giroux describes this damage: "No longer seen as a crucial social investment for the future of a democratic society, youth are now demonized by the popular media and derided by politicians looking for quick-fix solutions to crime. In a society deeply troubled by their presence, youth prompt in the public imagination a rhetoric of fear, control, and surveillance" (Giroux 554). Steve's story occurs in historical relation to the Omnibus Crime Bill and "tough on crime" efforts, including "broken window" policing and "stop and frisk," as overreach that result in over-policing/overreach and school-to-prison pipeline, arrest/sentencing disparities, other ways that perpetuate racism, especially against Black male youth.

Steve's scripting counters the overdeterminism with key choices that leave ambiguity. In his notes about the decisions on representing his involvement, he explains: "I thought about writing about what happened in the drugstore, but I'd rather not have it in my mind" (128). In this way, Steve's audience never gets the full story about what he saw in relation to the actual shooting. Steve places himself outside the scene in which the store owner loses his life because Steve did not identify with the crime: "I can see me at that moment, just when Mr. Nesbitt knew he was going to die, walking down the street trying to make my mind a blank screen" (128). Using filmic metaphors, he describes his emotional state after leaving his post as "look-out" as "blank," leaving room for possible innocence on both developmental and incidental levels.

In the exchange in which he becomes involved at Marcus Garvey Park in Harlem, Steve reveals his lack of clear understanding: "KING: Yeah, well you know, I found where the payday is. You know what I mean?" "STEVE: Yeah, I guess" (149). Steve is in the position where he wants to appear that he is savvy but does not really have a clear sense of what he is getting into for himself. Steve's position as an adolescent and an artist is very important here. Risk-taking and peer pressure are key aspects of adolescent development, and artists share a heightened sense of curiosity and desire to explore. What does that mean in this context? Susan Groenke notes:

> One consequence of the uneven distribution of the adolescent label is that some youth get to "act like teenagers" and others don't. As we know, for too many youth of color, "acting like teenagers" can result in increased surveillance, tracking into remedial courses and special education at school, school suspensions, incarceration, and loss of life. The deaths of Michael Brown, Trayvon Martin, and Jordan Davis confirm this, as does the "school-to-prison pipeline" that funnels youth of color out of public schools and into juvenile and criminal justice systems. (37)

When the film represents the moment of accountability, Steve leaves a gap: "CUT TO: CU of STEVE looking away. CUT TO: CU of KING. 'So what is it?' This phrase is repeated as the camera moves farther and farther away, growing louder and louder as STEVE and KING become tiny figures in the bustling mosaic of Harlem" (151). Steve as the filmmaker does not include his response in his script. With this delay, he is signaling his ambivalence at the time and as an artist representing the event. He also compels his audience into the space of ambiguity in relation to his "character" STEVE.

The script exposes the continuous reinforcement of visual cues to establish guilt from innocence, particularly in the courtroom, such as when the eyewitness for the prosecution, Lorelle Henry, testifies: "Camera swing to the rear of the courtroom" for her entrance. She is described as a "diminutive 58-year-old retired school librarian." She is "neatly dressed" and "was once a beautiful woman and is still quite attractive." "She moves with grace" (161). Briggs questions Mrs. Henry about the photographs of possible defendants she looked at while at the police station. Mrs. Henry had witnessed an argument involving a man she identified as James King with Mr. Nesbitt in which King demanded to know where Nesbitt kept the drugstore money. When Bobo Evans, another witness for the prosecution, enters the courtroom, his attorney complains about his appearance and the way that it may lead the jury: "Why is he dressed in his prison uniform? The prosecution is trying to connect him to my client. With him in prison gear, that prejudices my client" (172). Steve's alleged involvement in the crime was an accused "look-out" who gave "a sign . . . that everything was cool" (178–79), a gesture that has the potential to generate multiple readings, depending on the audience. Petrocelli enquires about Steve's role in giving the "all-clear signal" and asks if he offered any clear information, to which the witness replies: "He was supposed to tell us if there was anybody in the drugstore.

He didn't say nothing so we figured it was all right" (182), further illustrating the ambiguity.

In one of the final moments of his courtroom script, his teacher, Mr. Sawicki, takes the stand as a character witness. He has known Steve for three years in the film club and provides Steve with some hope that he will be recognized: "Then I had to write down the people who I admire. I wrote down Mr. Sawicki's name twice" (204). Mr. Sawicki's testimony stands in for a shift in viewing Steve that focuses on how Steve shapes his own world through the visual realm and makes meaning from his world: "I think he's an outstanding young man. He is talented, bright, and compassionate. He's very much involved with depicting his neighborhood and environment in a positive manner" (235). When asked if it is a stretch to consider Steve's filmmaking as relevant to the criminal case: "No, it's not. His film footage shows me what he's seeing and, to a large extent, what he's thinking. And what he sees, the humanity of it, speaks of a very deep character" (236). Unlike Johnnas's teacher, who reinforces limitations on Johnnas's creative gifts, Mr. Sawicki's testimony underscores the violence of a system that judges Steve precipitously. If the visual field marks Steve and becomes something he must overcome to avoid association with criminality, Mr. Sawicki shows the visual field, through the creative process of filmmaking, as a site to counter dehumanization: "It is my belief that to make an honest film, one has to be an honest person. I would say that. And I do believe in Steve's honesty" (237). The teacher's testimony asserts Steve's full humanity.

The trauma of incarceration has isolated him when he returns home after his acquittal as well. He is a changed person, but his artistic drive remains intact and thriving. The saving grace of the documentary production is that it allowed him to externalize the way others viewed him. He became very aware of himself as the subject of expectations, projections, and stereotypes. Critical consciousness developed and exhibited through the film. Through his scripting, he has engaged in a restorative process like the one described by Shawn Ginwright:

> Radical healing encourages reflection on personal issues and social conditions in order to develop political awareness and social action. This strategy provides insight into an *ecologically responsive* approach to working with black youth. . . . Radical healing as an ecologically responsive strategy highlights (1) the socially toxic conditions in urban communities, (2) the process for building the capacity for youth to respond to these conditions, and (3) the ways in which social justice, agency, and resistance can contribute to individual, community, and broader social wellness. (147)

Ginwright indicates the imperative for Black youth to see clearly the forces that try to erase their individuality and then remain detached or keep this process from taking over one's inner life through critical analysis, which in Steve's case takes the form of documentary filmmaking.

When faced with the personal crisis, he often returns to his mentor and the lessons he learned about controlling his narrative:

> CUT TO: FILM CLASS. MS of MR. SAWICKI. . . . "There are a lot of things you can do with film, but you don't have an unlimited access to your audience. In other words, keep it simple. You tell the story; you don't look for the camera technician to tell the story for you. When you see a filmmaker getting too fancy, you can bet he's worried either about his story or about his ability to tell it." (214)

The next part transitions into Steve using a "split-screen" device to capture O'Brien and Steve now before testimony. O'Brien tells him:

> You're going to have to take the stand—look at the jury and let the jury look at you—and say that you're innocent. . . . I know you'd better put some distance between yourself and whatever being a

tough guy represents. You need to present yourself as someone the jurors can believe in. Briggs isn't going to put King on the stand. That helps you, but when he sees us separating you from him, he's going to realize his client is in trouble. (216)

Respectability and association played out here. Steve's innocence must be established by distancing himself from someone who "reads" as a criminal in the eyes of the jury.

Photograph stills on pages 220–21 appear to show Steve in the drugstore with "What was I doing?" and then "What was I thinking?" in handwritten notes next to the images. These notes leave ambiguity as to their purpose. Steve may be questioning himself regretfully, or he may be reflecting as a director would on the character's motivations and experience as he discusses the issue of truth with another inmate. Steve tells the other inmate: "Truth is truth. It's what you know to be right" (221). Inmate 2 on the floor in the cell responds with the reality of prison life: "Nah! Truth is something you gave up when you were out there on the street. Now you talking survival. You talking about the chance to breathe some air 5 other guys ain't breathing" (222). This exchange challenges his documentarian view of recording an absolute truth, and instead looking at the truth allows for survival within these harsh circumstances. Steve's exchange suggests his movement toward the point at which documentary becomes art rather than reporting.

In Steve's questioning, he answers clearly and directly that he was not at the drugstore on the date of the robbery and did not serve as a lookout (223–24). During cross-examination, Steve becomes less definitive in his responses, indicating that he does not remember speaking with King at all in December. Any conversation he had with King was so insignificant as to be unmemorable. He was occupied with creating the film. His mind is always in filmmaker mode, even on the day of the crime. Steve tells Petrocelli that his memory of that time period entails planning for his film: "I don't know exactly where I was when the robbery took place. Most of the day I was going around taking mental notes about places I wanted to film for the school project" (231). He is confident and certain when discussing his process: "I don't even remember where I was. When the detectives asked me where I was, I couldn't even remember the day they were talking about," but he states that he knows that he was immersed: "I know because I was planning to do the film of my neighborhood over the holidays" (232).

Filmmaking allows him an escape from the courtroom and the fear he feels about the possible verdict. His creativity becomes a strategy for remaining calm and centered.

> Nothing is real around me except the panic. The panic and the movies that dance through my mind. I keep editing the movies, making scenes right. Sharpening the dialogue. "A getover? I don't do getovers," I say in the movie in my mind, my chin tilted slightly upward. "I know what is right, what truth is. I don't do tightropes, moral or otherwise." I put strings in the background. Cellos. Violas. (271)

In the final courtroom that Steve directs, he as a character in his own film is declared "not guilty." O'Brien, who has defended his innocence throughout the trial/film rejects his attempt to hug her at the verdict. "Her lips tense; she is pensive. She gathers her papers and moves away as STEVE, arms still outstretched, turns toward the camera. His image is in black and white, and the grain is nearly broken. It looks like one of the pictures they use for psychological testing, or some strange beast, a monster. The image freezes as the last words roll and stop mid screen" (276–77). In "'Tell Us How It Feels to Be a Problem': Hip Hop Longings and Poor Young Black Men," Imani Perry explains:

> In the United States today, perhaps no one is made to feel like a problem more acutely than the poor young Black man who, despite his great social vulnerability, is so often presumed to be a predator

or a threat. These youths proclaimed to be "in crisis" by commentators ranging from academics to *New York Times* headlines, respond to the question, "How does it feel to be a problem?" in the lyrics of our popular music. (165)

Steve, as a burgeoning filmmaker, addresses this question through his scripting and process notes. He captures his experience and the clear distinction that exists between Steve's consciousness of his actions and his developmental stage when he asks: "What did I do? What did I *do*? Anybody can walk into a drugstore and look around. Is that what I am on trial for? I didn't do nothing! I didn't do nothing! But everybody is just messed up with pain. I didn't fight with Mr. Nesbitt. I didn't take money from him" (115). However, his naivete does not save him from the judgment. Through his notes and journals, he reveals his youthful perspective and its unraveling as he encounters the brutality of the justice system. His scripting allows him to fashion some meaning from the chaos that leaves him questioning and estranged from his previous connections, as he indicates in his notes about his new normal at home: "My mother doesn't understand what I am doing with the films I am making. I have been taking movies of myself. In the movies I talk and tell the camera who I am, what I think I am about. Sometimes I set up the camera outside and walk up to it from different angles. Sometimes I set the camera up in front of the mirror and film my reflection" (281). Thinking back to O'Brien's turning away from him in the end, he asks at the book's closing: "What did she see?" (281). Steve joins all of the child artists who navigate their adolescence and incorporate the way they come into consciousness about the racialized identity to shape their art. Their stories incorporate a self-awareness that realizes the promise of "young, gifted, and black" at the site where it meets the imposition of "at risk" adolescence.

EPILOGUE

In a video project titled "How Does It Feel to Be a Problem?" University of Alabama student A. J. James responds candidly to the camera: "It's a strange thing to feel invisible, not in the metaphorical Ralph Ellison way . . . to actually walk around campus knowing that people have this sharpened ability to look right through you. It's feeling and knowing that people have the convenience of ignoring the complexities of your identities" (How Does It Feel to Be a Problem?). In the words of Felicia DeHaney, PhD, president and CEO of the National Black Child Development Institute: "We celebrate and cherish our children. They are not risks, but rewards. We believe that the true state of the Black child lies in their natural curiosity, excitement and genius, and we believe that they will indeed walk forward in the light." Or as poet Hafizah Geter writes, "I know, too, that though we lace our children with fear, we also flood them with possibility. We daisy-chain them in our lore. All our miracles have a Black child's face" ("Giving Up the Ghost"). Johnnas, Jimmy, Alexis, Precious, Abdul, and Steve are the "young souls" whom Amiri Baraka (LeRoi Jones) advises: "First, feel, then feel, then / read, or read, then feel, then / fall, or stand, where you / already are." These portraits of young Black artists have been celebrated here for their gifts to create and question, to place "at risk" any racist paradigms that narrow their horizons.

EPILOGUE

BIBLIOGRAPHY

Introduction

Capshaw, Katharine. *Civil Rights Childhood: Picturing Liberation in African American Photobooks.* U of Minnesota P, 2014.

Collins, Patricia Hill. *From Black Power to Hip Hop: Racism Nationalism and Feminism.* Temple UP, 2006.

Dobbs, David. "Beautiful Brains." *National Geographic*, vol. 220, no. 4, Oct. 2011, pp. 36–59.

Henning, Kristin. "Criminalizing Normal Adolescent Behavior in Communities of Color: The Role of Prosecutors in Juvenile Justice Reform." *Cornell Law Review*, vol. 98, no. 2, 2013, pp. 383–461.

Rothenberg, Albert. "Creativity in Adolescence." *Psychiatric Clinics of North America*, vol. 13, no. 3, 1990, pp. 415–34.

Toldson, Ivory A. "Why It's Wrong to Label Students 'at-Risk.'" *The Conversation*, 11 Feb. 2021, theconversation.com/why-its-wrong-to-label-students-at-risk-109621.

Chapter 1: "On the Verge of Flying Back": The Problematic of the Young, Gifted, and Black Artist in Bill Gunn's *Johnnas*

Baldwin, James. "Sweet Lorraine (1969)." Introduction. *To Be Young, Gifted and Black,* by Lorraine Hansberry, Vintage Books, 1995.

Barnes, Clive. "'Black Picture Show,' a Tale of Corruption." *New York Times*, 7 Jan. 1975, www.nytimes.com/1975/01/07/archives/black-picture-show-a-tale-of-corruption.html.

Barris, Kenya. "Black-Ish/Sink or Swim." Season 2, episode 14, ABC, 10 Feb. 2016.

The Black Power Mixtape 1967–1975. Orland Park, IL: MPI Home Video, 2011.

Breslin, Jessica. "'If I Were White, I'd Be Better Off.'" *Sojourners*, 7 May 2015, sojo.net/articles/if-i-were-white-id-be-better.

Brewster, Joe, et al., directors. *American Promise.* Ro*Co Films Educational, 2013.

Brooks, Daphne A. "Nina Simone's Triple Play." *Callaloo*, vol. 34, no. 1, 2011, pp. 176–97. *Project MUSE*, https://doi:10.1353/ca1.2011.0036.

Bullins, Ed. "The King Is Dead." *The Drama Review: TDR*, vol. 12, no. 4, 1968, pp. 23–25. *JSTOR*, https://doi.org/10.2307/1144375.

Capshaw, Katharine. *Civil Rights Childhood: Picturing Liberation in African American Photobooks*. U of Minnesota P, 2014.

Chokshi, Niraj. "Racism at American Pools Isn't New: A Look at a Long History." *New York Times*, 1 Aug. 2018. NYTimes.com, www.nytimes.com/2018/08/01/sports/black-people-pools-racism.html.

Diawara, Manthia, and Phyllis R. Klotman. "Ganja and Hess: Vampires, Sex, and Addictions." *Black American Literature Forum*, vol. 25, no. 2, Summer 1991, p. 299. *EBSCOhost*, doi:10.2307/3041688.

Dore, Rebecca A., et al. "Children's Racial Bias in Perceptions of Others' Pain." *British Journal of Developmental Psychology*, no. 2, 2014, p. 218. *EBSCOhost*, https://doi:10.1111/bjdp.12038.

Du Bois, W. E. B. *The Souls of Black Folk; Essays and Sketches*. A. G. McClurg, 1903. New York: Johnson Reprint Corp., 1968.

Forster, Nicholas. "What Took You and Everyone Else So Long to Write about Gunn?!" *Black Film Center Archive Blog*, 16 July 2018, blogs.iu.edu/bfca/2018/07/16/what-took-you-and-everyone-else-so-long-to-write-about-gunn/.

Franklin, Raymond S. "The Political Economy of Black Power." *Social Problems*, vol. 16, no. 3, 1969, pp. 286–301. *JSTOR*, https://doi.org/10.2307/799663.

Geary, Daniel. "The Moynihan Report: An Annotated Edition." *The Atlantic*, 14 Sept. 2015, www.theatlantic.com/politics/archive/2015/09/the-moynihan-report-an-annotated-edition/404632/.

Goyal, M. K., et al. "Racial Disparities in Pain Management of Children with Appendicitis in Emergency Departments." *JAMA Pediatrics*, vol. 169, no. 11, 2015, pp. 996–1002, https://doi:10.1001/jamapediatrics.2015.1915.

Grantham, T.C. "Creativity and Equity: The Legacy of E. Paul Torrance as an Upstander for Gifted Black Males." *Urban Review*, no. 45, 2013, pp. 518–38, https://doi.org/10.1007/s11256-013-0257-2

Gunn, Bill. *Black Picture Show*. Reed Cannon & Johnson Pub, 1975.

Gunn, Bill. *Ganga and Hess*. Kelly-Jordan Enterprises, 1973.

Gunn, Bill. "Johnnas." *The Drama Review: TDR*, vol. 12, no. 4, 1968, pp. 125–38. *JSTOR*, https://doi.org/10.2307/1144393.

Gunn, Bill. "To Be a Black Artist," *New York Times*, 13 May 1973, pp. 121, 144, www.nytimes.com/1973/05/13/archives/to-be-a-black-artist-a-black-artist-.html.

Harris, Ida. "Why I View Childish Gambino's 'This Is America' as Black Art Imitating White Fantasies." *Blavity News*, 15 May 2018.

Hoffman, Kelly M., et al. "Racial Bias in Pain Assessment and Treatment Recommendations, and False Beliefs about Biological Differences between Blacks and Whites." *Proceedings of the National Academy of Sciences of the United States of America*, vol. 113, no. 16, 2016, pp. 4296–301.

Bibliography

King, Woodie, Jr. "Black Theatre: Present Condition." *The Drama Review: TDR*, vol. 12, no. 4, 1968, pp. 116–24. *JSTOR*, https://doi.org/10.2307/1144392.

Krasner, David. "Rewriting the Body: Aida Overton Walker and the Social Formation of Cakewalking." *Theatre Survey*, vol. 37, no. 2, Nov. 1996, pp. 67–92.

Labrie, Peter. "The New Breed." *The Negro Digest*, vol. 15, no. 9, July 1966. Reprinted in *Black Fire: An Anthology of Afro-American Writing*, edited by Amiri Baraka and Larry Neal, Black Classic Press, 1968, pp. 64–77.

Moore, Alicia L., and La Vonne I. Neal. "Foreword: 'Young, Gifted, and Black: Keeping Your Soul Intact.'" *Black History Bulletin*, vol. 73, no. 1, 2010, pp. 4–6. *JSTOR*, www.jstor.org/stable/24759659.

Neal, Larry. "The Black Arts Movement." *The Drama Review: TDR*, vol. 12, no. 4, 1968, pp. 28–39. *JSTOR*, https://doi.org/10.2307/1144377.

Peterson, Louis. *Take a Giant Step: A Drama in Two Acts*. S. French, 1954.

Robinson, Danielle. "'Oh, You Black Bottom!' Appropriation, Authenticity, and Opportunity in the Jazz Dance Teaching of 1920s New York." *Dance Research Journal*, vol. 38, no. 1–2, 2006, pp. 19–42.

Rosemond, Ebony. "This Stereotype Is Killing Black Children." *Washington Post*, 10 Feb. 2017, www.washingtonpost.com/opinions/this-stereotype-is-killing-black-children/2017/02/10/2c06fa14-e249-11e6-a547-5fb9411d332c_story.html.

Ryfle, Steve. "The Eclipsed Visions of Bill Gunn." *Cineaste*, vol. 43, no. 4, Fall 2018, pp. 26–31.

Semmes, Clovis E. *Roots of Afrocentric Thought: A Reference Guide to Negro Digest*. Greenwood Press, 1998.

Sharpe, Christina Elizabeth. *In the Wake: On Blackness and Being*. Duke UP, 2016.

Sloan, A. S. "A Forecast for Blackness: The Work of Victor LaValle." *Callaloo*, vol. 33, no. 4, 2010, pp. 979–81, 1154.

Stewart, James T. "The Development of the Black Revolutionary Artist." *Black Fire: An Anthology of Afro-American Writing*, edited by Amiri Baraka and Larry Neal, Black Classic Press, 1968, pp. 3–11.

Turner, Rob. "Childish Gambino's This Is America Video: An Analysis." *Creative Review*, 9 May 2018, www.creativereview.co.uk/childish-gambinos-this-is-america-an-analysis/.

Whiting, G. W. "From at Risk to at Promise: Developing Scholar Identities among Black Males." *Journal of Advanced Academics*, vol. 17, no. 4, 2006, pp. 222–29.

Ziya, Hari. "Black People Still Can't Swim: Reflections on the McKinney, TX Pool Incident 3 Summers Later." *The Black Youth Project*, 4 June 2018.

Chapter 2: "My Portrait Is Gold": Resiliency and the Crisis of the Black Child's Image in Dael Orlandersmith's *The Gimmick*

Akbar, Maysa. *Urban Trauma: A Legacy of Racism*. Purpose Driven Publishing, 2017.

Alexander, Jeffrey C. "Toward a Theory of Cultural Trauma." *Cultural Trauma and Collective Identity*, edited by Bernard Giesen et al., U of California P, 2004, pp. 1–30.

Bost, Darius, et al. "Introduction: Black Masculinities and the Matter of Vulnerability." *The Black Scholar*, vol. 49, no. 2, 2019, pp. 1–10, https://doi:10.1080/00064246.2019.1581970.

Breslau, Naomi, et al. "Traumatic Events and Posttraumatic Stress Disorder in an Urban Population of Young Adults." *Archives of General Psychiatry*, vol. 48, no. 3, Mar. 1991, pp. 216–22.

Brown, August. "Young Rappers Are Getting Honest about Doing Battle with Depression, Drug Addiction and Suicide." *Los Angeles Times*, 25 Jan. 2018, www.latimes.com/entertainment/music/la-et-ms-hip-hop-depression-2018 0128-story.html.

Coleman, Chris. "On Beating the Odds." *American Theatre*, vol. 16, no. 7, Sept. 1999, p. 32.

Collins, Patricia Hill. *From Black Power to Hip Hop: Racism Nationalism and Feminism*. Temple UP 2006.

Cross, Dorthie, et al. "Childhood Trauma, PTSD, and Problematic Alcohol and Substance Use in Low-Income, African-American Men and Women." *Child Abuse & Neglect*, vol. 44, June 2015, pp. 26–35.

Dayton, Tian. *Trauma and Addiction: Ending the Cycle of Pain through Emotional Literacy*. Health Communications, 2000.

Elliot, Jeffrey, and Charles White. "Charles White: Portrait of an Artist." *Negro History Bulletin*, vol. 41, no. 3, 1978, pp. 825–28. *JSTOR*, www.jstor.org/stable/44213837.

Fabre, Michel. *From Harlem to Paris: Black American Writers in France, 1840–1980*. U of Illinois P, 1993.

Funkhouser, G. Ray. "Trends in Media Coverage of the Issues of the '60s." *Journalism Quarterly*, vol. 50, no. 3, 1973, pp. 533–38.

Graham, Hugh Davis. "On Riots and Riot Commissions: Civil Disorders in the 1960s." *The Public Historian*, vol. 2, no. 4, Summer 1980, pp. 7–27.

Harold, Christine, and Kevin Michael DeLuca. "Behold the Corpse: Violent Images and the Case of Emmett Till." *Rhetoric and Public Affairs*, vol. 8, no. 2, 2005, pp. 263–86. *JSTOR*, www.jstor.org/stable/41939982.

hooks, bell. *Art on My Mind: Visual Politics*. New Press: W. W. Norton, 1995.

Khoury, Lamya et al. "Substance Use, Childhood Traumatic Experience, and Posttraumatic Stress Disorder in an Urban Civilian Population." *Depression and Anxiety*, vol. 27, no. 12, 3 Dec. 2010, pp. 1077–86, https://doi:10.1002/da.20751.

Labrie, Peter. "The New Breed." *The Negro Digest*, vol. 15, no. 9, July 1966. Reprinted in *Black Fire: An Anthology of Afro-American Writing*, edited by Amiri Baraka and Larry Neal, Black Classic Press, 1968, pp. 64–77.

Lorde, Audre. "Poetry Is Not a Luxury." *Sister Outsider: Essays and Speeches* (Crossing Press Feminist Series). Crossing Press, 2007, pp. 36–39.

McDowell, Deborah E. "Recovery Missions: Imaging the Body Ideals." *Recovering the Black Female Body: Self-Representations by African American Women*, edited by Michael Bennett and Vanessa D. Dickerson, Rutgers UP, 2001, pp. 296–318.

Mitter, Siddhartha. "'What Does It Mean to Be Black and Look at This?' A Scholar Reflects on the DANA Schutz Controversy." *Hyperallergic*, 25 Mar. 2017, hyperallergic.com/368012/what-does-it-mean-to-be-black-and-look-at-this-a-scholar-reflects-on-the-dana-schutz-controversy/.

Orlandersmith, Dael. *The Gimmick. Beauty's Daughter, Monster, The Gimmick: Three Plays*. Penguin Random House, 2000.

Patton, Stacey. "Why Are We Celebrating the Beating of a Black Child?" *Washington Post*, 1 May 2015, www.washingtonpost.com, www.washingtonpost.com/opinions/2015/05/01/cca770dc-ef9f-11e4-a55f-38924fca94f9_story.html.

Raiford, Leigh. *Imprisoned in a Luminous Glare: Photography and the African American Freedom Struggle*. U of North Carolina P, 2011.

Richardson, Elaine B. *African American Literacies*. Routledge, 2003.

Spence, Lester K. *Knocking the Hustle: Against the Neoliberal Turn in Black Politics*. Punctum Books, 2015.

Stafford, Zach. "Exhibit of Michael Brown's Death Scene 'Atrocious,' Activists Say." *The Guardian*, 14 July 2015, www.theguardian.com/artanddesign/2015/jul/14/white-artist-recreation-scene-michael-brown-death-divides-opinion.

Stovall, Tyler Edward. *Paris Noir: African Americans in the City of Light*. Houghton Mifflin, 1996.

United States. *Report of the National Advisory Commission on Civil Disorders*. U.S. Government Printing Office, 1968.

Wilson, Judith, "Getting Down to Get Over: Romare Bearden's Use of Pornography and the Problem of the Black Female Body in Afro-U.S. Art." *Black Popular Culture*, edited by Gina Dent, Bay Press, 1992, pp. 112–22.

Woodhouse, Barbara Bennett. *Hidden in Plain Sight: The Tragedy of Children's Rights from Ben Franklin to Lionel Tate*. Princeton UP, 2008.

Youth in the Ghetto: A Study of the Consequences of Powerlessness and a Blueprint for Change by Harlem Youth Opportunities Unlimited, Inc. 1964.

Chapter 3: Posttraumatic Literacies and the Material Body in Sapphire's *Push*

Bhuvaneswar, C., and A. Shafer. "Survivor of That Time, That Place: Clinical Uses of Violence Survivors' Narratives." *Journal of Medical Humanities*, vol. 25, 2004, pp. 109–27, https://doi.org/10.1023/B:JOMH.0000023175.21955.dc.

Boylorn, Robin. "Unbreakable or the Problem with Praising Blackgirl Strength." Crunk Feminist Collective, 23 July 2014, www.crunkfeministcollective.com/2014/07/22/unbreakable-or-the-problem-with-praising-blackgirl-strength/.

Brunzell, Tom, et al. "Teaching with Strengths in Trauma-Affected Students: A New Approach to Healing and Growth in the Classroom." *American Journal of Orthopsychiatry*, vol. 85, no. 1, 2015, pp. 3–9.

Chen, Caroline. "Sapphire, Author of Push and the Kid: AIDS Has Hit African Americans 'as Hard as Slavery.'" *SF Weekly*. SF Weekly, February 24, 2020. archives.sfweekly.com/exhibitionist/2011/07/06/sapphire-author-of-push -and-the-kid-aids-has-hit-african-americans-as-hard-as-slavery.

Cooper, Brittney. "'Maybe I'll Be a Poet, Rapper': Hip-Hop Feminism and Literary Aesthetics in 'Push.'" *African American Review*, vol. 46, no. 1, 2013, pp. 55–69.

Dagbovie-Mullins, Sika A. "From Living to Eat to Writing to Live: Metaphors of Consumption and Production in Sapphire's Push." *African American Review*, vol. 44, no. 3, 2011, pp. 435–52, https://doi:10.1353/afa.2010.0018.

David, Marlo D. "'I Got Self, Pencil, and Notebook': Literacy and Maternal Desire in Sapphire's Push." *Tulsa Studies in Women's Literature*, vol. 35, no. 1, June 2016, pp. 173–99, https://doi:10.1353/tsw.2016.0019.

Davis, Kai, et al. "Sandra Bland." *Button Poetry*, 22 May 2016, www.youtube.com/ watch?v=QpSC_IusogI. Accessed 1 June 2019.

Giroux, Henry A., et al. "Henry A. Giroux: Can Democratic Education Survive in a Neoliberal Society?" *Truthout*, 16 Oct. 2012, truthout.org/articles/can-democratic -education-survive-in-a-neoliberal-society/.

Hillsburg, Heather. "Compassionate Readership: Anger and Suffering in Sapphire's Push." *Canadian Review of American Studies*, vol. 44, no. 1, Apr. 2014, pp. 122–47, muse.jhu.edu/article/541837.

King, Tiffany Lethabo. "Black 'Feminisms' and Pessimism: Abolishing Moynihan's Negro Family." *Theory & Event*, vol. 21, no. 1, 2018, pp. 68–87. *Project MUSE*, muse.jhu.edu/article/685970.

Klein, Rebecca. "A Year after the Assault at Spring Valley, One Student Turns Her Pain into Progress." *HuffPost*, 2 Feb. 2017, www.huffpost.com/entry/spring -valley-high-school_n_5807b9a1e4b0b994d4c35881.

"Let Her Learn: A Toolkit to Stop School Push Out for Girls of Color." National Women's Law Center, 6 Nov. 2018, https://nwlc.org/resource/let-her-learn -a-toolkit-to-stop-school-push-out-for-girls-of-color.

McConnico, Neena, et al. "A Framework for Trauma-Sensitive Schools." *Zero to Three*, vol. 36, no. 5, May 2016, pp. 36–44.

McDowell, Deborah E. "Recovery Missions: Imaging the Body Ideals." *Recovering the Black Female Body: Self-Representations by African American Women*, edited by Michael Bennett and Vanessa D. Dickerson, Rutgers UP, 2001, pp. 296–318.

McNeil, Elizabeth. "Un-'Freak'ing Black Female Selfhood: Grotesque-Erotic Agency and Ecofeminist Unity in Sapphire's Push." *MELUS: Multi-Ethnic Literature of the U.S.*, vol. 37, no. 4, Nov. 2012, pp. 11–30, https://doi:10.1353/ mel.2012.0070.

McNeil, Elizabeth A., et al. "'Going After Something Else': Sapphire on the Evolution from *Push* to *Precious* and *The Kid*." *Callaloo*, vol. 37, no. 2, 2014, pp. 352–57, 465, 467–68.

Muhammad, Gholnecsar E. "Searching for Full Vision: Writing Representations of African American Adolescent Girls." *Research in the Teaching of English*, vol. 49, no. 3, 2015, pp. 224–47. *JSTOR*, www.jstor.org/stable/24398701.

Perry, Bruce D. "Fear and Learning: Trauma-Related Factors in the Adult Education Process." *New Directions for Adult and Continuing Education*, no. 110, 8 June 2006, pp. 21–27.
Rountree, Wendy. "Blues, Hope, and Disturbing Images: A Comparison of Sapphire's Push and the Film *Precious*." *Presenting Oprah Winfrey, Her Films, and African American Literature*. Palgrave Macmillan, 2013, pp. 161–78. https://doi.org/10.1057/9781137282460_7.
Statman-Weil, Katie. "Creating Trauma Sensitive Classrooms." *Young Children*, vol. 70, no. 2, 2015, pp. 72–79.
Taylor, Kate. "At Success Academy, a Stumble in Math and a Teacher's Anger on a Video." *New York Times*, 12 Feb. 2016, nyti.ms/1mwgqz9.
Wallace, Michele. *Invisibility Blues: From Pop to Theory*. New ed., Verso, 2008.
Weems, Renita. "'Artists without Art Form': A Look at One Black Woman's World of Unrevered Black Women." *Home Girls: A Black Feminist Anthology*, edited by Barbara Smith, Kitchen Table/Women of Color Press, 1983, pp. 94–105.

Chapter 4: "My Body of a Free Boy . . . My Body of Dance": Violence and the Choreography of Survival in Sapphire's *The Kid*

Bakewell, Danny J. "State: How Many of the Victims were Black?" *Chicago Defender*, Nov. 2011, arktos.nyit.edu/login?url=https://www-proquest-com.arktos.nyit.edu/newspapers/penn-state-how-many-victims-were-black/docview/915826853/se-2?accountid=12917.
Everett, Julin. "The Postcolonial Orphan's Autobiography: Authoring the Self in Jamaica Kincaid's 'Mr. Potter' And Calixthe Beyala's 'La Petite Fille Du Réverbère.'" *College Literature*, vol. 36, no. 3, 2009, pp. 45–65.
Gale, Daryl. "Race Beside the Point in PSU Case." *Philadelphia Tribune*, 18 Nov. 2011, p. 1.
Herman, Judith. *Trauma and Recovery: The Aftermath of Violence—from Domestic Abuse to Political Terror*. Basic Books, 1992.
Jackson, Lawrence M. "The Black Male Dancer Physique: An Object of White Desirability." *Journal of Pan African Studies*, vol. 4, no. 6, 2011, pp. 75–81.
Jülich, Shirley. "Stockholm Syndrome and Child Sexual Abuse." *Journal of Child Sexual Abuse*, vol. 14, no. 3, 2005, pp. 107–29.
Martin, Crystal G. "A Mother's Power: *Precious* Author Sapphire Discusses *The Kid*." *O: The Oprah Magazine*, Aug. 2011, www.oprah.com/omagazine/sapphire-author-interview-qa-with-sapphire-the-kid-push-sequel. Accessed 29 Aug. 2013.
Monteiro, Nicole M., and Diana J. Wall. "African Dance as Healing Modality throughout the Diaspora: The Use of Ritual and Movement to Work through Trauma." *Journal of Pan African Studies* vol. 4, no. 6, 2011, pp. 234–52.
Rich, John A. *Wrong Place, Wrong Time: Trauma and Violence in the Lives of Young Black Men*. Johns Hopkins UP 2009.
Roberts, Dorothy. *Shattered Bonds: The Color of Child Welfare*. Basic Books, 2002.

Sapphire. *Push*. Vintage, 1997.
Sapphire. *The Kid*. Penguin, 2011.
Smith, Joan. "Misery by the Bucket Load." *Sunday Times*, 4 Sept. 2011, p. 56.
Woodhouse, Barbara Bennett. *Hidden in Plain Sight: The Tragedy of Children's Rights from Ben Franklin to Lionel Tate*. Princeton UP, 2008.

Chapter 5: "You're Young, You're Black, and You're on Trial. What Else Do They Need to Know?": Reading Walter Dean Myers's *Monster*

Anderson, Elijah. Introduction. *Against the Wall: Poor, Young, Black, and Male*. U of Pennsylvania P, 2008, pp. 1–27.
Beardsley, Kathryn, and Carrie Teresa. "The Journey from 'Just Us' to Some 'Justice': Ideology and Advocacy, the *New York Amsterdam News*, and the Central Park Jogger Story." *American Periodicals: A Journal of History & Criticism*, vol. 27 no. 2, 2017, pp. 165–79. Project MUSE, muse.jhu.edu/article/668549.
Bennett, William John, et al. *Body Count: Moral Poverty—and How to Win America's War against Crime and Drugs*. Simon & Schuster, 1996.
Bernstein, Robin. *Racial Innocence: Performing American Childhood and Race from Slavery to Civil Rights*. New York UP, 2011.
Boghani, Priyanka. "They Were Sentenced as 'Superpredators.' Who Were They Really?" *Frontline*, PBS, 2 May 2017, www.pbs.org/wgbh/frontline/article/they-were-sentenced-as-superpredators-who-were-they-really/.
Brown, Elizabeth. "'It's Urban Living, Not Ethnicity Itself': Race, Crime and the Urban Geography of High-Risk Youth." *Geography Compass*, vol. 1, no. 2, 2007, pp. 222–45.
Byfield, Natalie P. *Savage Portrayals: Race, Media, & the Central Park Jogger Story*. Temple UP, 2014.
Calamur, Krishnadev. "Ferguson Documents: Officer Darren Wilson's Testimony." *NPR*, NPR, 25 Nov. 2014, www.npr.org/sections/thetwo-way/2014/11/25/366519644/ferguson-docs-officer-darren-wilsons-testimony.
Capshaw, Katharine. *Civil Rights Childhood: Picturing Liberation in African American Photobooks*. U of Minnesota P, 2014.
DuVernay, Ava (@ava). "Not thugs. Not wilding. Not criminals. Not even the Central Park Five. They are Korey, Antron, Raymond, Yusef, Kevin. They are millions of young people of color who are blamed, judged and accused on sight." 1 Mar. 2019. 7:07 a.m. Tweet.
Feeney, Michael, and Ginger Adams Otis. "Central Park Five—Wrongfully Convicted in 1989 Rape—Settle with City for $40 Million." *Nydailynews.com*, 20 June 2014, www.nydailynews.com/new-york/nyc-crime/central-park-40m-settlement-article-1.1836991.
Fleetwood, Nicole R. *Troubling Vision: Performance Visuality and Blackness*. U of Chicago P, 2011.

Giroux, Henry. "Racial Injustice and Disposable Youth in the Age of Zero Tolerance." *International Journal of Qualitative Studies in Education*, vol. 16, no. 4, 2003, pp. 553–65.

Gonnerman, Jennifer. "Kalief Browder, 1993–2015." *The New Yorker*, 3 Oct. 2017, www.newyorker.com/news/news-desk/kalief-browder-1993-2015.

Greenberg, Zoe, et al. "City Releases Trove of Documents in Central Park Jogger Case." *New York Times*, 20 July 2018.

Groenke, Susan L., et al. "Disrupting and Dismantling the Dominant Vision of Youth of Color." *The English Journal*, vol. 104, no. 3, 2015, pp. 35–40. *JSTOR*, www.jstor.org/stable/24484454.

Johnson, Sheri Lynn, et. al. "The Pre-Furman Juvenile Death Penalty in South Carolina: Young Black Life Was Cheap." *South Carolina Law Review*, vol. 68, no. 3, 2016, p. 331.

Lott, Tommy Lee. "Documenting Social Issues: Black Journal, 1968–1970." *Struggles for Representation: African American Documentary Film and Video*, 1999, pp. 71–98.

Marable, Manning. "From Freedom to Equality: The Politics of Race and Class." *Soul: Black Power, Politics, and Pleasure*, edited by Monique Guillory and Richard Green, New York UP, 1998.

Mathias, Christopher. "Here's Kalief Browder's Heartbreaking Research Paper on Solitary Confinement." *HuffPost*, 23 June 2015, www.huffpost.com/entry/kalief-browder-solitary-confinement-research-paper_n_7646492.

Mueller, Benjamin, et al. "City Releases Trove of Documents in Central Park Jogger Case." *New York Times*, 20 July 2018, www.nytimes.com/2018/07/20/nyregion/documents-from-the-central-park-jogger-case-are-released.html.

Myers, Walter Dean. *Monster*. HarperCollins, 1999.

Perry, Imani. "'Tell Us How It Feels to Be a Problem': Hip Hop Longings and Poor Young Black Men." *Against the Wall: Poor, Young, Black, and Male*, edited by Elijah Anderson, U of Pennsylvania P, 2008.

Shook, Jeffrey J. "Contesting Childhood in the US Justice System: The Transfer of Juveniles to Adult Criminal Court." *Childhood*, vol. 12, no. 4, 2005, pp. 461–78.

Sullivan, Ronald. "2 Teen-Agers Are Convicted in Park Jogger Trial." *New York Times*, 12 Dec. 1990, NYTimes.com.

Taylor, Keeanga-Yamahtta. *#BlackLivesMatter to Black Liberation*. Haymarket Books, 2016.

Thomas, Jeree. "Two-Years After Kalief Browder's Death States, Begin to Reform Youth Criminal Justice." *HuffPost*, 6 June 2017, www.huffpost.com/entry/remembering-kalief-browder-the-state-of-youth-in-adult_b_59371d25e4b04ff0c4668280?section=us_black_voices.

Welch, Michael, et al. "Moral Panic Over Youth Violence: Wilding and the Manufacture of Menace in the Media." *Youth & Society*, vol. 34, no. 1, Sept. 2002, pp. 3–30, https://doi:10.1177/0044118X02034001001.

Williams, Patricia J. "Lessons from the Central Park Five." *The Nation*, vol. 296, no. 18, May 2013, p. 9.

Epilogue

Baraka, Amiri. "Young Soul." *The Oxford Anthology of African-American Poetry*, edited by Arnold and Hilary Herbold, Oxford UP, 2006, p. 202.

Geter, Hafizah. "Giving Up the Ghost: There Are a Million Ways to Teach a Black Boy about Death." *Yale Review*, June 18, 2020, https://yalereview.org/article/giving-ghost.

Ginwright, Shawn. *Black Youth Rising: Activism and Radical Healing in Urban America*. Teachers College Press, 2010.

Maddox, Patrick, director. Amanda Bennett, AJ James, and Elliot Spillers, writers. *How Does It Feel to Be a Problem*. *Vimeo*, 19 Aug. 2022, https://vimeo.com/prmaddox/howdoesitfeel.

INDEX

abuse, sexual, 84, 122, 124, 128, 130
Adams Otis, Ginger, 151
adolescence, 6–7, 9–10, 18, 33, 52, 93, 166–67, 174; development, 4, 6, 92, 132, 168
agency, 5, 7, 73, 76, 87, 91, 123, 125, 128, 133, 137, 142, 147; creative, 153, 157
AIDS epidemic, 89
Akbar, Maysa, 53–54, 63
Alexander, Jeffrey C., 48
Amsterdam News, 161
Anderson, Elijah, 148
art, visual, 57, 63, 119
artistic development, 11, 21, 34, 38, 53
Atlanta Child Murders, 4, 66

Bakewell, Danny, 129–30
Baldwin, James, 8, 14, 45, 54–56, 58–59, 74, 76
BAM (Black Arts Movement), 22, 26, 34
Baraka, Amiri, 175
Barnes, Clive, 21–22
Beardsley, Kathryn, 160
Bennett, William John, 145
Bhuvaneswar, Chaya, 93
bias, 50, 146; adultification, 95; Black children's pain, 32; confirmation, 152; implicit, 36, 39; racial, 160
Black artist, 4, 7–8, 13–44, 56
Black Arts Movement (BAM), 22, 26, 29, 34

Black bodies, 26, 32, 71; explicit, 64
Black children, 7, 16, 27, 32, 38, 41, 43, 50, 66, 81, 151–52
Black child's image, 46–78, 151
Black female nude in art, 68
Black-ish, 27
Black Lives Matter, 145
Black pain, 32, 60, 63
Black Power Mixtape, The, 16
Black Youth Project, 5
Black Youth Rising, 5
Bland, Sandra, 116
Bost, Darius, 60–61
Boylorn, Robin M., 115
brains, teenage, 85–86, 165
Bridges, Ruby, 3, 16, 80
broken window policing, 167
Brooks, Daphne A., 30
Browder, Kalief, 155–56
Brown, August, 60
Brown, Michael, 4, 10, 65, 143, 150, 168
Bruce, La Marr Jurelle, 60–61
Bullins, Ed, 15
Burns, Ken, 146
Byfield, Natasha, 145

cakewalking, 24
Capshaw, Katharine, 3–4, 19
Carmichael, Stokely, 16
Central Park Five, 10, 145–46, 157
Childish Gambino, 24

Index

civil rights era, 3–5, 8, 13, 15, 45, 48, 57, 80, 88, 115, 144–45
civil rights movement, 16, 48, 65, 109
classroom community, 80, 82, 107, 116, 154
Clinton, Hillary, 144
Coleman, Chris, 47
Coleman-King, Chonika, 166
collective identity, 17, 23, 34, 37
Collins, Lisa, 68–69
Collins, Patricia Hill, 3, 66, 86
Color Purple, The, 96, 101–2, 109–10
Combs, Jasmine, 116
consciousness, 33, 36, 149, 174; new, 18; political, 34; womanist, 112
Cooper, Brittney, 88–89
creativity, 7, 25, 38–39, 43, 45, 54–55, 73, 75, 77, 108, 110–11, 117, 120
Crenshaw, Kimberle, 80
cultural trauma, 48
culture wars, 5, 80, 108, 160; mid-nineties, 81

David, Marlo D., 101
Davis, Jordan, 143, 168
Davis, Kai, 116
Day, Carol Brunson, 3
DeHaney, Felicia, 175
dehumanization, 10, 24, 99, 145, 157
DeLuca, Kevin Michael, 64
Diawara, Manthia, 23
DiJulio, John J., Jr., 145
dissociation, 91; media-supported, 89; traumatic, 88, 97, 101, 105, 132
Dobbs, David, 6
documentary, 38–39, 146, 149, 172; documentarian, 157, 172; documentary production, 170; documentary realism, 153
Donaldson, Elizabeth, 102
Du Bois, W. E. B., 13
DuVernay, Ava, 157

Eckford, Elizabeth, 16
education, gifted, 38
estrangement, 54, 56, 61, 71, 73, 86, 147, 164
Everett, Julin, 135
Exonerated Five, 144–45, 161. *See also* Central Park Five

Feeney, Michael, 151
Ferguson, Missouri, 10, 150. *See also* Brown, Michael; Wilson, Darren
filmmaking, 153, 170, 173
Fleetwood, Nicole, 150
Forster, Nicholas, 22
Franklin, Aretha, 110
Franklin, Raymond S., 22–23
freedom, artistic, 35, 41, 75, 96

Gale, Daryl, 130
Ganja & Hess, 17
Geary, Daniel, 18–19
Georgetown Law School's Center on Poverty and Inequality, 94
Geter, Hafizah, 175
giftedness, 35, 37, 70, 105, 147
Ginwright, Shawn, 171
Giroux, Henry A., 94, 167
Gonnerman, Jennifer, 157
Goyal, M. K., 32
Graham, Hugh Davis, 49
Grantham, T. C., 38
Gray, Freddie, 50
Groenke, Susan L., 167, 168
Gunn, Bill, 4, 7–8, 13, 17, 19, 22–23

Hansberry, Lorraine, 8, 14, 59
Harold, Christine, 64
Harlem, 45–46, 48, 51, 53, 55–56, 58, 70–71, 90, 109, 112, 168–69
Harlem Youth Opportunities Unlimited, 76
Harlins, Latasha, 4
Harris, Ida, 25

Index

Haughton, Tanya, 161
healing, 76, 107, 139; intertextual, 141; healing force, 67
Henning, Kristin, 6–7
Herman, Judith, 132
hip-hop feminism, 88
HIV, 110, 111, 125
Hoffman, Kelly M., 32
hooks, bell, 57, 59
Hughes, Langston, 90, 100, 109, 112, 115, 141
hypervigilance, 84, 163
hypervisibility, 48, 66; hypervisibility-invisibility, 81; paradoxical, 158

"I am Trayvon Martin" campaign, 150
integration, 14–16, 18–19, 23, 27, 35, 38, 81; shattered bus window, 81
Isom, Lisa, 161

James, A. J., 175
Jim Crow, 40
Johnson, Sheri Lynn, 151, 152
Jones, Bill T., 137
Jones, Nayo, 116
Jülich, Shirley, 130

Kenny, Niya, 79–80. *See also* McKinney pool incident
Kerner Commission report, 48–49, 144
King, Martin Luther, Jr., 15
King, Tiffany Lethabo, 97
King, Woodie, Jr., 21
Klotman, Phyllis R., 33
Krasner, David, 24

Labrie, Peter, 44, 52
legacy, 21, 24–26, 38, 48, 53, 56, 61, 65, 100, 107, 140
literacy, 82, 91–93, 95, 97, 101, 106, 108, 117, 121, 135
Long Wharf Theatre, 45
Lott, Tommy Lee, 144

Manning, Brandon J., 60–61
Marable, Manning, 151
Martin, Crystal G., 119
Martin, Trayvon, 4, 143, 168
masculinity, 41, 61, 160
McCone Commission, 49
McDowell, Deborah E., 68, 87
McKinney pool incident, 27. *See also* Kenny, Niya
McKissick, Floyd, 15
McNeil, Elizabeth, 91
memory, 10, 64, 103, 114, 123–24, 137, 139, 141–42, 154, 172
Mensa, Vic, 60
Mobley, Mamie Till, 65. *See also* Till, Emmett
Monteiro, Nicole M., 139
Moore, Alicia L., 39, 43
moral panic, 49, 145–46
Morrison, Toni, 29, 102
Moynihan Report, 18–19, 30, 97
Mueller, Benjamin, 156

National Black Child Development Institute (NBCDI), 3, 175
National Women's Law Center, 79
Neal, Larry, 29
Neal, La Vonne I., 39, 43
Negro Digest, 33, 52
Negro Ensemble Company, 15
neoliberalism, 57, 94
new breed, 29
New Jim Crow, 145
New York Times, 21, 155, 174
nonviolence, 15–16

Omnibus Crime Bill, 144, 151, 167
Orlandersmith, Dael, 45, 47

pain assessment, 32
Patton, Stacey, 50
Perry, Bruce, 84–85
Perry, Imani, 173–74

poetry, 36, 51, 78, 91, 93, 95, 101–2, 112, 114–17
pool imagery, 101
posttraumatic experience, 65, 125, 135, 153, 157; posttraumatic counternarrative, 119; posttraumatic restriction, 117; posttraumatic symptoms, 114

Raiford, Leigh, 64
reparations, 128
response: posttraumatic, 5, 43, 84; stress, 85, 103
Rice, Tamir, 4, 66, 149
Rich, John A., 142
Richardson, Elaine B., 69
Robinson, Danielle, 24
Rosemond, Ebony, 27
Rothenberg, Albert, 7
Roundtree, Wendy, 102
Ryfle, Steve, 17, 22

Salaam, Sharrone, 161
Sapphire, 4, 9, 93, 95–96, 102, 119–20, 128, 130, 132, 138
school resource officers, 79, 95
school-to-prison pipeline, 81
Schutz, Dana, 65
segregated classroom, 80
segregated spaces, 61
Semmes, Clovis E., 33
Shafer, Audrey, 93
Sharpe, Christina, 32–33, 65
Simone, Nina, 29
Sloan, A. S., 43
Smith, Joan, 128
social worker, 98, 100, 103, 127
Spence, Lester, 57–58
Spring Valley Assault case, 80–82
Statman-Weil, Katie, 85
Stewart, James T., 44
Stinney, George, 143, 151
Stockholm Syndrome, 130
"super-predator," 144

"Sweet Lorraine," 8, 14, 56, 59
swimming, 26–27, 101, 123
system, social service, 97–98, 127, 135

Take a Giant Step, 17–18
Tate, Greg, 140
Taylor, Kate, 81
Taylor, Keeanga-Yamahtta, 145
teacher, 35–40, 43, 61, 82–85, 90, 113, 154, 166, 170
Teresa, Carrie, 160
thinking, divergent, 7, 51, 91, 117
Till, Emmett, 64
Toldson, Ivory A., 4
trauma, 30, 32–33, 49, 52, 80, 82, 85, 89, 91, 93, 113, 115; and addiction, 75
trauma-informed classrooms, 113
Turner, Rob, 25

Urban Trauma, 53–54, 63

visibility/visual, 66, 88, 104, 114, 140; fragmented, 120; racialized, 164; visual cues, 169; visual elements, 155; visual field, 170

Walker, Aida Overton 24
Walker, Alice, 100, 102, 109, 111–12, 141
Wall, Diana J., 139
Wallace, Michelle, 96
Weems, Renita, 116
Welch, Michael, 146
White, Charles, 63, 67
white supremacy, 17, 20–21, 25, 34, 38
"wilding," 146, 148
Williams, Patricia, 146
Wilson, Darren, 149
Wilson, Judith, 68
Wise, Kharey/Khourey, 155. *See also* Central Park Five; Exonerated Five
witnessing, 52, 82, 107, 119, 158
Woodhouse, Barbara Bennett, 64

Ziyad, Hari, 27–28

ABOUT THE AUTHOR

Photo courtesy of the author

Jennifer Griffiths is a professor of English at the New York Institute of Technology. She is author of *Traumatic Possessions: The Body and Memory in African American Women's Writing and Performance.*

CPSIA information can be obtained
at www.ICGtesting.com
Printed in the USA
BVHW042207291122
652363BV00001B/8